From A Fatherless Father To His Sons

Andre D. Harrison

From A Fatherless Father To His Sons

Copyright © 2012 Andre D. Harrison

Cover Design, Cover Photo, Interior Photo by
Katrina Charles of T.C. Designs www.tcdesignzonline.com

Edited by Tiffani J. Knowles of NEWD Magazine www.newdmagazine.com

Unless otherwise noted, Scripture quotations are taken from The Holy
Bible, English Standard Version® (ESV®)
Copyright © 2001 by Crossway,
a publishing ministry of Good News Publishers.
All rights reserved.
ESV Text Edition: 2007

ISBN: **0615633706**
ISBN-13: **978-0615633701**

DEDICATION

I would like to dedicate this book first to God. He truly has brought me through a lot and given me the strength to press on. Second, to my sons Isaiah, Nathaniel and Gabriel. You three keep me on my toes and are my encouragement to be the best example of a man I can be. I LOVE YOU SO MUCH.

And to future children I may have, this book is also dedicated to you.

CONTENTS

ACKNOWLEDGMENTS

I would like to thank my mother, Gloria Harrison, for the sacrifices she made to raise me in the best way she could.

To my grandmother, Ina Harrison, the most beautiful woman in the world, who gave immeasurable support to my mother in raising me.

To my siblings, Alicia and Anton Harrison, for their support. And a special mention to Stacey Rivera and my brother Quinton Lowther.

To my editor Tiffani Knowles who was a much needed nag and an encourager for me to finish the book.

To the mother of my children Magalena Rodriguez, without her I would not be a father, thank you for giving me the three most amazing gifts a man can ever have.

To Gloria Rodriguez, her encouragement has been a springboard for me.

To Blinda Blair who made me believe that this was all possible from before the first word in the book was written, thank you.

To all the men mentioned in this book, thank you for being there for me.

To Pastor Hilda Ortiz for offering her fine-tooth comb services in reading this book.

To the National Fatherhood Initiative whose resources have been a help to me as I improve my role as a father in my kids' lives.

To my sons who have kept me on my toes and striving to be a better man. I love you so much.

I would also like to thank my biological father Irving Rivera. Even though he wasn't present in my youth, he is here now and we are building a strong relationship today.

Lastly, to my family and friends who have stuck by me to encourage me to finish this book. Your encouragement kept me going and I thank all of you. You all are greatly appreciated.

Andre D. Harrison

Introduction

As I sit on my bed writing, my nine-year-old son lies next to me watching *Fairly Odd Parents* on Nick Toons. In this moment, I can't help but reflect on what it is to be a man and what it takes to get there.

When I was nine, I never would have imagined that I would be lying in bed with one of my sons watching them watch television while I attempt to write a book. Yet and still, I am here. Thinking.

Even though I am a 31-year-old father, how do I know I have reached manhood yet? Am I even clear on what a man truly is?

As a father of three sons, I have the esteemed pleasure and pressure of rearing boys to become men. To teach them what is acceptable and unacceptable for a man. Pleasure, because I find it an honor that God sought fit to bless and entrust me with such a responsibility. Growing up, I did not have a father to show me how to become a man. Pressure, because I am the primary example to my sons of what a man should be.

I admit I am not perfect. I have a host of flaws. In fact, one of my greatest fears is that one day they'll look at me and think that I've failed as a man. Regardless of that fear, I write this -- mostly because I recognize that my sons deserve a father to show them how to be a man. They deserve a father who will leave with them the legacy of manhood.

Having an absentee father, I had to learn many lessons by trial and error. And despite having great men like my Uncle Jake, my Uncle Dwight, my Godfather Ralph, and my brother's father Alvin, I felt a constant void of not knowing who my father was, what my father was and why he wasn't there. The men I did know growing up had their own responsibilities, so their quality time with me was sporadic. I understood and, regardless, I knew their love for me.

I learned a lot from these men, but even still, I longed for a father to sit me down and explain to me what it meant to be a man. I longed for a father to teach me socially-acceptable behavior for a man. I longed for a father to show me how to interact with girls and teach me what appropriate conduct was when it came to being in a relationship with a woman. I longed for a father to talk to me about sex. I look back and ponder my past. Many of the mistakes I made could have been avoided simply by me having an active and consistent father, or father figure - for that matter.

It wasn't until I was 30 that the day I had longed for finally came. I came face to face with my biological father. I was nervous and anxious all at the same time. It was an amazing experience to see the other side of who I was. Questions of why flew through my mind but I kept the questions to myself. As excited as I was to meet him, I made sure not meet him with expectations of having a father-son relationship. My heart was actually guarded. Twenty-eight years had passed without him in my life, and I didn't want to set myself up for disappointment. I didn't need another man that was part-time in my life. If he couldn't be there to reestablish a relationship with us full-time, then just meeting him would suffice.

To be honest, both my twin sister and I felt slighted growing up without our father. Though our father wasn't present in our childhood, we were able to evade many of the big pitfalls that ensnare the young and fatherless. I am proud of us. Today, we are both striving to be positive role models for our own children and for the youth in our communities.

Presently, my father and I are building a strong relationship based on realistic expectations of one another. My sons now have the opportunity to know their grandfather and, for that, I am extremely grateful. The past is where it should be, behind us.

For years, men have been absent from witnessing the full development of their children -- be it because of occupation, hobbies, other personal interests, or lack of physical presence. As a result, mothers have had to take up this mantle -- unnaturally, of course.

The honest truth is a woman cannot teach a boy to become a man better than a man can teach a boy to become a man. Similarly, a man cannot teach a girl to be a woman better than another woman can.

The role of the man in the home has been made to diminish. Men are confused about what role they **should** play in their homes. Today's man, like me, has been taught by a woman to be a man. Many of these women harbor mixed motives – be it sometimes sub-consciously.

She wants to raise a man that isn't like the one who hurt her in the past. If she was physically abused by a man, then she may overpower her son, making him feel that a woman is boss. If her mate was lazy, she may be overly insistent about her son doing chores and hard labor, wearing him out. It goes even further than past hurts. She may want to a raise a son who fits her internal vision of who a perfect man is. Because the woman's idea of a perfect man is based on internal fantasies, she will either be too hard on the boy or too soft on the boy. In many ways, this plan backfires. The boy may become handicapped and may never reach his true potential in his manhood. Often times, this boy may set out to do exactly the opposite of his mother's requests in an attempt to resist the pressure to measure up to a mother's idea of manhood.

Sadly, many men who have endured a childhood like this have buckled under the pressure when they reach manhood. The cycle may repeat itself and he, in turn, becomes another absentee father. Their ignorance is not their fault. The fault lies with their absentee father. Some men would rather run than stand up and face the responsibilities that come with being a parent. In most cases, it was what their father did.

There is encouraging news despite the odds, however. A remnant. A few good men who have answered the call to be the best fathers they can be. I am among them. Men like myself stand firm in their commitment to being a consistent father in the lives of their children. I personally know men who have grown up with absentee fathers who are now amazing fathers. Their commitment shines brilliantly.

They are men just like me who were forced to learn how to become a man by trial and error, this book is for you.

It is also for boys who are currently searching for their manhood without the help of their fathers. Use this book as a guide. Whether your father left you as a child, works all the time, or passed away, use this to assist you on your journey.

If you are a father who wants to teach your sons how to be a man, this book can also be of help to you. It may not cover everything you need to know as a man, but it will most certainly put you on the right track.

Keep polishing your skills. Make your search for manhood a lifetime one and never forget to look to the Creator of Man to learn how to be a real man.

Finally, this book is for my three sons. Make this your manual for growing into your manhood. Many of these lessons I have already taught you. Some I have yet to teach you.

Enjoy this book.

Chapter 1 - Grow Up

- Growth is evidence of life

"Dead man walking, dead man walking" resounds in my mind every time I think about the movie the *Green Mile*. It follows the lives of men sentenced to death and the prison guards assigned to them. When a prisoner is walking from his cell to the execution chamber, the guards who are escorting the prisoner chant "dead man walking" through the halls. Allow me to re-appropriate that phrase. There are many "dead men walking" around every day, not sentenced to death by a jury, but sentenced to death because of a refusal to grow in their manhood. One of the major evidences of life is growth. Something that is alive grows. Something that is dead decomposes (rots), until there is nothing left.

- The journey of manhood is a lifelong journey filled with possibilities and opportunities for learning. The mistake we make as men is we believe that manhood should coincide with age. That notion is far from the truth. I know some 40-year-old adult males who have been out-manned by a 16-year-old who got a girl pregnant and chose to be a father to his child and a support to his child's mother.

Age is a number not a barometer for maturity.

In conversations with older men, I often hear this quote: "Young man, I am old enough to be your father." Most often the reason they use this saying is to prove that they pull rank.

So, in return, I say, "Cool. Well, **Dad**, I am running low on money today, so can I have $200 to pay my car note?" Usually, they laugh it off. But, the fact is, they usually do this to use age as a means of control and not just as a means of earning respect. Ironically, men who aren't present in their own children's lives have had the gall to us that line on me. I am not saying not to offer respect to those who are your elders, but a wise man always considers the source of the information they are receiving.●Deadbeat parents usually offer advice without offering support. How is a "dead man" going to give a "living man" advice on being a man? Later on, I dedicate a chapter to acting on your word. ●

Physical growth is a natural part of life but what is learned are the qualities that make an "alive" man. These qualities are developed. You're not born with them. Whatever qualities you use the most will become stronger, while the others will become weaker. If you desire the qualities that make a good man, a man that is alive, then you must practice those qualities continually.

So the question is, how do I learn which qualities need developing?

You have made the first step by picking up this book. I applaud you.

● Next, you must find a trusted father figure. Look for a father figure who possesses manly qualities. He should have quiet strength.●He shouldn't have to tell you that he possesses these qualities. He should simply exhibit them.●This father figure will admit that he still has a lot to learn in becoming a man.●In fact, this is the proof that he is looking to mature, to grow as a man. It is also further proof that he is a man who is alive. If a man gives you the impression that he has arrived at completion, my advice to you is RUN. More than likely, he is a man who is decomposing, and just as decomposing fruit can ruin fruit around it, a decomposing man can ruin you.

You have one of two choices to make. The first is, you can choose to be a man who is alive, one who is consistently growing, or the second, you can be a man who is dead and unconcerned with development.

"I call heaven and earth to witness against you today, that I have set before you life and death, blessing and curse. Therefore choose life, that you and your offspring may live!" **-Deuteronomy 30:19**

These two are set before you: life and death, and I beg you, as a man seeking growth, that you choose life.

* You can't be a boy forever

When I was a kid, one of my favorite commercials advertised my favorite store and the jingle went like this:

"I don't want to grow up, I'm a Toys 'R' Us kid, there's a million toys at Toy 'R' Us that I can play with, from bikes to trains to video games, it's the biggest toy store there is, I don't want to grow up because if I did, I wouldn't be a Toys 'R' Us kid."

I quoted that from memory. Yes, I remembered that song from my childhood. In short, that jingle asserts our number one issue. Some men have refused to grow up because they still desire to be a child who isn't responsible for anything or anyone. There are men living alone without a steady mate because they do not want the responsibilities of being a man. They want to have boyish fun forever. Everyone reaches a point where they look back over their lives and examine what they have done. If you live your life looking just to have fun, party and do the things that are expected of an adolescent, then when you reach 50 years old you will look back at your life wondering why you have nothing to show for it. You will feel like a failure as a man. And, you'd be right.

The ultimate failure is to not have produced, created or developed anything at all. That's the epitome of a dead man walking.

Perfect ex.

Other cultures, that some may even call primitive, seem to better understand the importance of a boy becoming a man. These cultures have implemented practices that divided boyhood from manhood.

A ceremony common among many North American native tribes was coined the "vision quest" by anthropologists in the 19th century.

This ceremony is performed as a rite of passage for adolescent males, but not exclusively so. It begins when a boy of 14 or 15 years of age is brought into the sweat lodge. There, his body and spirit are purified by the heat from the burning of cedar. Inside the sweat lodge there is a medicine man who is present to advise and assist him with his prayers. Afterwards, he is taken to an isolated spot and left there to fast for four days. There he will pray, contemplate the words of the medicine man, and await a vision which will reveal to him his path in life as a man in native society (Heinrich, Corbine, & Thomas, 1990).

The sole purpose is to teach the boy that he could not be a boy forever. Some of these practices were so severe that the boy would have to pass this test to prove his manhood or literally die trying.

I am reminded of the movie *300*. Every man in that province became a man because they underwent rites of passage to achieve this rank. Rites of passage are a set of rituals that mark a person's progress from one status to another: in this case, a boy to a man. (Sidenote: *300* is the greatest movie ever next to *The Sound Of Music* and *Lean On Me*.)

300 commences with the main character, King Leonidas, as a youth undergoing his rites of passage. At age seven, he is taken from his mother and plunged into a world of violence being forced to fend for himself. He must do what it takes to survive. Leonidas is punished by rod and lash to teach him how a man must endure pain, sometimes with no mercy. Then, he is sent into the wilderness to survive. He either would come back a Spartan Man or not at all. *300* depicts, in my opinion, King Leonidas as a very balanced man. He is one who loves his wife, loves his children, loves his kingdom and is willing to fight and give his life for each.

When I was 13, I had the opportunity to attend a classmate's bar mitzvah. In Judaism, a bar mitzvah is a ceremony and festive event that celebrates a young man's transition from boyhood to manhood. I had a great time, but remembered thinking how much I wanted something like that for me.

• Regrettably, what is pushed by modern media is the belief that the celebration of a boy's transition to manhood today is sex. That is not a rites of passage by any means or a celebration of manhood. Some fathers pat their sons on the back for losing their virginity. That type of affirmation cripples a boy's growth because it warps his idea of what a man is. We will discuss that later on.

No matter how old, you need to understand that being a boy forever is unacceptable. Your interests have to change as you grow into manhood. If you are still interested in the same childish things as you were when you were 17, 12 or 8, then you have to reevaluate how much you've grown as a man. This is not to pass judgment, but to stress that the interests of a boy should not be the same as those of a man.

• Men are interested in those who are around them while boys are interested in themselves. Men seek to provide while boys seek provision. Men rise to a challenge while boys retreat to something easier. Men seek to create while boys seek to copy. •

Where do you measure up on the scale from boys to men? Here is the great part about it. You will never need to reach the end of the scale because you have to keep in mind that you will always be growing into manhood. There are no perfect men, including myself. I am writing this book so that as I grow as a man I can also encourage my sons and others to grow as men.

- Maturity is a part of growing up

No one is born with the ability to act in a mature manner. Maturity is developed. One who is mature is one who has achieved a low but stable growth rate. This person has enough humility to realize that he is in a lifelong process of growth. This person has enough humility to realize that perfection is worth pursuing even if it's unattainable.

Maturity is a funny thing because it may vary from one person to another. People can perceive maturity very differently. As for me, actions speak louder than age. For one to be mature, they must take up certain responsibilities. My sons show me their level of maturity when they do something wrong, tell me the truth about it and accept responsibility for their action. Every time my sons do wrong and they accept responsibility, I praise them because it is a sure sign of maturity.

Healthy maturity is gradual growth. There is nothing wrong with being young, as long as you are seeking to mature yourself. When I was 17, I was all about basketball. In fact, my good friend Matthew Reeves introduced me to Christ by inviting me to play basketball at his church gym.

One evening, a preacher from England came to the church with a 17-year-old young man who was also from England. We invited him to the gym to play basketball with us and we were shot down by these words, "Basketball. Please...that is for children." I stopped short in amazement. I thought he was so mature.

Our youth pastor, Pastor Lawrence Hallahan, later told me, "Andre there is nothing wrong with being young, and basketball isn't a children's sport."

Instantly, that brought me comfort. There I was thinking this 17 year old from England, who wore a shirt and tie as casual wear, was mature for his age. If you truly seek maturity, you will find it. Still, it is important to learn the balance of fun and maturity and where the lines should be drawn.

- The Balance of Fun and Maturity

Anyone that knows me knows that I love to have fun. I am a goof ball when I want to be and I encourage those around me to have fun, too. The teens in my youth ministry do not know what to make of me doing the latest dances at a Sweet 16, when I joke around with them, when I talk junk on the basketball court, or play video games fairly skillfully. It's also funny to see the older people in the church cock their heads when I rock to the Electric Slide at a wedding. Some may say I am a big kid; however, I merely understand how to balance fun and maturity.

For some, maturity is solely based on appearance. Example: I can drive a CL-Class Benz, wear designer three-piece suits with cuff links, and an official Rolex and some may see me and think I am mature. But what they may not know is that I am unmarried, have 6 kids by 5 different women, don't pay child support and I live in the basement of my parents' home. Is that a mature man?

Some Christians think that if I pray loudly, speak in tongues, shout "Praise God" at the appropriate times, then I am spiritually mature. On the contrary, if I do those things, it may not be that I am spiritually mature, it may mean that I have rehearsed them so well that it appears that I am mature. I am actually putting on an act for those on the outside. Sometimes I do not fit the mold of what many would consider to be a mature man because of my childlike heart and energy, but inside I am seeking maturity beyond my years and appearance. I want to encourage you not to seek to look mature but to be mature -- despite what people may say.

Being young at heart doesn't make you less of a man; it just means you enjoy life. What's the sense in being a man who is alive and you not enjoy the life you are trying to live? Men break because they are forced to uphold this persona of manly maturity forced upon them by their mothers or grandmothers. They will use phrases like "Grow Up" or "Be a man." When a boy is having fun, these phrases serve to stifle them and cause them to become unbalanced. In many cases, these men will tilt to one side of the spectrum.

My Uncle Dwight is a huge example of what it means to balance fun and maturity. Since I was a kid, I could remember Uncle Dwight taking all the kids to Prospect Park or Seaside Heights on summer Saturdays. He was energetic and fun all while being responsible. Uncle Dwight worked with my mother for a couple of years. I remembered going into work and seeing him with his work hat on. He showed me what fun and maturity was.

Balance is a major force of life; without it the universe will fall out of tilt. The scale of life will not balance itself. It is up to you to find the balance and apply it. I had to find this balance on my own. I asked myself, what kind of fun could I have that would not damage my growth as a mature man? What you do for fun is just as important as how you have fun. Every man needs their time of recreation, even the "older" and more "mature" men. If you like to play sports, cards, fish or even play with building blocks, make sure you balance your fun and recreation with a sense of responsibility. You can do this by making sure your priorities are in order.

- Prioritize Properly

"The LORD detests double standards; he is not pleased by dishonest scales." - **Proverbs 20:23 NLT**

● Poor priorities have been a plague among men for generations and it's the reason many grown males fall short of becoming men.●Understanding the importance of priorities at a young age will set you up for sure growth as a man.● Knowing where to place things in your life on the scale of importance is a key component to growth.● It's difficult for boys to understand how to prioritize because, in some cases, the men in their lives are not being a good example at it. Every man should have his priorities in order; if he doesn't, he is merely a boy. Men seek to line up the things and people in his life in order of importance to him. Everyone has priorities but some do not have healthy priorities or their priorities in the right places. If you want to grow from one stage to the other, you must prioritize properly.

My senior year in high school was the worst year in my educational career. I had messed up my sophomore and junior years so bad (I hadn't found God until the end of my junior year). Prior to my spiritual re-focusing, my priorities were out of whack. School was number four on the list behind girls, money, and fun.

During my sophomore and junior years in high school, I reaped the consequences for my poor prioritizing. Senior year came and I sat with my guidance counselor about what I needed to do to graduate. She read me a long list of classes I had to make up in one year; needless to say, I had no life my senior year. With the help of God and a few key people in my life, I was able to graduate on time. I had to reestablish my priorities to ensure I would grow to the next stage in my life. Lesson: establish priorities that will set you up for growth.

Priority isn't a grown up word. It's not something that old people do. Everyone does it whether they realize it or not. If you know that you have chores to do and you decide to play video games instead of doing what is responsible, then you have just set a priority. Even though your priorities are poor, they are still priorities. If I worked all summer and used the money to buy a new pair of Jordans instead of paying for books I need in my course of study, then my priorities are also poor. Even at a young age, boys have to learn how to prioritize properly. Even now, I like to get a little video gaming in with my sons. But, I will not sacrifice cooking a meal for my kids so I can play a video game.

I heard it like this from my old friend Mr. Joseph when he commented on my Facebook page one day: *"Prioritizing goes hand in hand with sacrifice. Very important."*

Setting right priorities will save you from tons of headaches as you grow into manhood. This is what I believe a man's priorities should look like:

1. God

God comes before all things. To acknowledge and serve the Creator is to do all the things that follow on the list below. The most important person in anyone's life has to be the Creator of all things because, if it wasn't for Him, we would not exist. Furthermore, if it wasn't for the sacrifice of His Son, we would not be redeemed from all the sins we commit as men.

2. Self/Wife

Notice how I put these two together. As a married man, your spouse's needs must become your needs, as well. In every culture, marriage symbolizes the union of two individuals. So, you are no longer just YOU, you have become US. Taking care of your spouse is just as important as taking care of yourself. If you are unmarried, you must place yourself right under God. Even though a man considers others above himself, he must ensure that he is capable of doing just that. Keep yourself healthy and strong. When you fly on an airplane, the flight attendants explain to you that in the event that the oxygen masks drop, you must first secure your mask before helping another. You are of no use to anyone dead. Remember, we seek to be men that are alive.

> ***Side Note*** *–If you are a child of a step parent, you must understand that if your mother or father puts your step parent before you on their list of priorities, then they are doing the right thing. If that step parent is mistreating you in any way,*

though, tell your mother or father immediately.

3. Children

I do not care what your present life situation is. Your children must come before all the other items that follow. Falling short on this is not an option; you are not a man if you do not put your children near the top of your list of priorities. We will be getting to this later in the book, but here is a taste of things to come. Your children are your legacy. They are what you will leave behind. Children are entrusted to us by God to love, nurture, care for and guide and every child needs their father to play those roles in their lives. If you do not have children, you should still learn this because one day it will apply. One of the worst things for a child is to feel as if they come second to an occupation, a friend or even obligations at church or service to others. The church begins in your home and your congregants are your children; they need to be served first.

4. Family

This is where people may disagree, and on this, I am open for discussion. The first three are locked in. On those points, I will not compromise. But these next few are a little bit more flexible. Your family is a part of who you are, your generation. I love to see close families. If your extended family is close and healthy, then the priorities that follow become much easier to tackle because of the support of said family. My brother's father, Alvin, had a family with such a close bond. No family is perfect but the bond that this family is my example of a close-knit and supportive family. Take me, for instance. We are not related by blood but, if ever I needed something, they are all there for me. So imagine what they will do for those who actually share in their gene pool.

5. Occupation/School

A job and school go hand in hand in this priority. An occupation is the principal business of one's life; so if you are in school, your business is to excel in it. School to a 16-year-old man has to be just as important as work is to a 40-year-old man. Many men take occupation and they put it at the top of this list, before God, Self/Wife, and their Children. The result is a chaotic life with no direction for his family. Even though a man's job helps to provide for his family, it should never become more of a priority than the relationship he has with his wife and children. This I learned many years ago. I had to tell myself I would rather argue with my boss about the amount of extra hours I am not working then argue with my wife about the amount of extra hours I do work. If possible, don't just look for a job that will put food on the table and clothes on your backs, but look for a job that understands the importance of family. If that isn't possible, then start your own business. Make your own hours so you can make your family a priority and even teach your family the business. Just make sure that the business will support your family.

6. Friends

- I'll start with this. If any person you consider a friend doesn't encourage you in any of the previous five priorities, then they truly aren't friends of yours. • Friends want the best for you and will look to support you in your priorities. It is very hard for a male to find a close friend that he considers a confidant, so when they find that friend they try to stick with him for life. This is a good thing unless this friend encourages you to forsake your previous priorities. A friend that doesn't respect your priorities may sound like this:

"Hey, let's hit up the club tonight."

"Yo, that girl is checking you out. Go talk to her. "What your wife doesn't know won't hurt her."

"So what if you have your kid's recital? This is game 7 of the NBA finals."

"You were so much more fun before you found God."

"Skip work and let's hit the beach or skip school and let's go get into something."

If you have heard anything of the sort from a so-called friend, then it's time for you to cut them out of your life or at least draw boundaries around your relationship so that you can persist in your growth as a man. Friends ought to offer support and help. There are friends of mine who I could go for months without speaking to, and when we do speak, our relationship picks up as if there was no lapse in time. The support is always there. Remember that friends are the family that you choose, so make sure you choose them wisely.

7. Church/Service To Others

You may be wondering why I put this last or why God and Church are separated out on my list of priorities. Let me explain. I do not feel a man's relationship with God should revolve around a church building or even his service to the church. A good church can help build your relationship with God but should never be the basis of the relationship. I firmly believe your relationship with God is most important at home. Most people spend an average of two hours in a church weekly, which means that out of the 168 hours in a week an average of two of those hours are spent in a church. A good church will support the priorities found above, and if you are attending a church that teaches you that they are the center of your life and you must give everything to them, then I suggest you leave and find a good family-friendly church that teaches healthy priorities for men. When I was ordained into ministry, a woman told me something I will never forget. She said, "Please do not be like my father. He is a good man but he put the church before his family and it hurt us all." I will take that saying to my grave. Men, you may feel you are doing God a service by making church your priority, but in actuality you are hurting the very ones God has entrusted you as a man to take care of first. Young men, learn from that example and make sure that you do not hurt your family in service to the church. That will never be God's expectation of you.

Healthy priorities are important for every man who wants to grow in their manhood. Every great man has his priorities straight.

- Chapter Summary

Being a man is a state of mind and of action. It is not based on the number of years you have been living on the earth. You may have lived 35 years but you can still be a "dead man walking." A man who is truly alive is a man who is growing in his manhood. •Never settle for the idea that once you are 18, you have achieved manhood. You can be 6 feet tall, with a full beard and hair on your chest and still be a boy. If that is the case, you are nothing but a dead man walking. Seek to grow as a man from here on out. No matter if you are reading this at age 12 or 72. Growth is the proof that you are a "Man Alive." ◑

Chapter 2 - Look the Part and Be the Part

- What Does A Man Look Like

My perception of a man didn't come from my father. The last memory I had of him was my mother holding me while standing at the top of the staircase of our East New York, Brooklyn apartment. He was standing at the bottom. I was too young to remember the conversation between him and my mother but I do know it wasn't a pleasant one. That was the last day he saw us and we saw him before our reunion in September of 2010.

For the son of an absentee father, the perspectives about men are developed based on what is seen outside of the home -- if there isn't a stepfather or older sibling present. Sons of absentee fathers are handicapped in a way. We don't automatically understand what a man should look like because there isn't a man there to look up to. Our understanding can become skewed.

For a child, the idea of a man is based on a favorite cartoon or comic book hero. As he reaches his pre-teen years, the idea of what a man looks like is usually framed by conversations with peers. At that age, he isn't looking for heroes. He's looking to be a man. It is a transitional period for him. In his adolescent years, he continues to look to his surroundings to find out what a man looks like. Society and media play a huge role in his perception.

Let's examine the hero search first. When I was 6, I would have constant squabbles with other boys my age about how my father's muscles were bigger than theirs. By father, I meant my brother's father, Alvin. Alvin was the first father figure I can remember growing up. When he would come by, I vividly remember waiting on my bed for him, and as soon as he walked in the room, I would jump on his back. My mother told me I had to stop doing that when I reached 12 years old and I was almost his height. I wanted to be like him, to look like him, to walk like him... because he was what a man looked like to me. I loved Alvin and till this day we have a great relationship. Unnaturally, still, I had to look to another man who wasn't my father to learn what a man should look like. Yet, I was fortunate to have Alvin in that stage of my life.

At 16, Alvin wasn't around as often as he once was, but he was always a phone call away. I began to struggle between what I saw men looked like in the neighborhood growing up and my Uncle Jake. If my Uncle Jake wasn't there, I would have no doubt developed a pretty lengthy rap sheet.

Some of the men in the neighborhood growing up didn't have any direction. As often as I went outside, there were men sitting aimlessly on a bench, drinking alcohol and smoking marijuana. The men that did have direction weren't visible because they were usually in their homes doing the right thing. Back then, the right thing to do was to simply stay out of trouble.

These men on the bench usually were unshaven, had unkempt hair and wore clothing that didn't match or was altogether filthy. However, these were the men that took time to talk with me as a youth; they were always there.

Watching them holler at women as they walked by (funny enough, many times the women actually responded), hearing their profanity-laced speech, listening to their arguments with their "baby mommas," picking up the stench of alcohol and weed on their persons, and watching the way they earned money by slinging dope was normal. But, were these acts the normal behavior of a man? It wasn't much different from the behavior of men I saw in the rap videos growing up.

From watching Biggie, Tupac, Method Man, Redman, Slick Rick and others on TV, I assumed that this was what it took to be a successful man. These rappers appeared to have money, cars, clothes and the girls. I never got close enough to any of them to confirm how they smelled, though. Still, I never strived to be a rapper even though that was how I thought one could attain success as a man. I thank God for the contrast found in my Uncle Jake.

My Uncle Jake was the exact opposite of that imagery. He was a college graduate and a teacher before going into law enforcement. I never heard a word of profanity slip from his mouth and he took care of his children. My Uncle Jake also possessed this innate "swag." When he entered the room, his 6'4" slender frame and pleasant, clean-cut handsome looks always lit up the environment around him. He was a giant to me, but so smooth. Like a ninja, he would creep up in the most unsuspected places, surprising you with a hello.

When I was 14, I was in an awkward stage in my life. I had long braids, an earring and would wear my pants below my waist from time to time. That is what the idle men in my neighborhood looked like. My mother was under a lot of pressure and wasn't in a position to show me what a man looked like, nor was it her place. My uncle saw the earring when I first got it and shared his disappointment with me. He often told me that I looked like a girl with my braids; he also told me that if he ever saw me with my pants sagging that he would break my arm. Uncle Jake was a student of Aiki-Jujitsu so I believed him.

As a youth, I was definitely confused about what a man should look like. My uncle didn't live with me and he wasn't my father. I do believe that it would have been much different had my father been present. Instead of wearing sagging pants, braids and an earring, I probably would have been wearing Cuban-style button up shirts with a fedora and matching slacks. This is what my father calls fashion today.

- Hygiene: Clean, Cut and Shaven

A man should desire to look clean and presentable no matter his haircut or style of dress. A grungy look isn't acceptable for a man unless you are home or just got finished with a grueling sports match. Maturity is a state of mind and you should determine to always look clean and presentable.

From time to time, we would have sleep overs at our church for teens called "lock-ins." Although we don't have showers in our church, I would make it clear to the youth that they must bring with them a wash cloth, toothbrush, toothpaste and deodorant. Even a homeless man will go into a public bathroom, wet paper towels and clean himself off. And regardless of the advertisement, spraying yourself with *Axe* will not make you smell good if you do not first clean your body.

Adolescent boys tend to forget that they are getting older and a stench that has been tactfully coined as "B.O." (Body Odor) seeps from their underarm. You must shower and wash your body thoroughly from head to toe. Wash your hair, too. A hat doesn't cover the stench. It only enhances it because the scent gets into the fabric. Wash your neck, so the collars on your shirts don't stain with dead skin. Scrub down your underarms and your pubic areas. When you are using the bathroom and are releasing stools, make sure to wipe properly, and yes, scrub that area too when you shower.

Drinking juice or using mouth wash are not substitutes for brushing your teeth. Even though they may eliminate the morning breath feel, they don't eliminate the morning breath smell. Trust me. Dental hygiene goes far beyond the smell. At least twice a day you must brush your teeth. Once you wake up in the morning, take your toothbrush and brush every area of your mouth, up down, left right, and in circles. Do the same in the evening to remove the particles of food that collect between your teeth during the day. This helps prevent decaying teeth. Then, use mouth wash to help rinse away additional waste.

As your body grows, so will the amount of hair on your body. This means that you will have hair in places you never knew hair could grow. It's not like a plant that needs the sun. Hair will grow in dark places. Trimming the hair there makes it easier to clean those areas. This is completely your choice, but I do suggest it. Please be careful and maybe consult a physician on the safest way to do it.

Many have the ability to cut their own hair. I am not one of those people. I make an effort to go to the barber bi-weekly to get my haircut and I never let my hair go more than a month before a haircut. Another possibility is buying a set of clippers to cut your hair to the length you want it. Then, go to the barber for an inexpensive line-up. This will definitely cut the cost of having to pay top price for a haircut.

Shaving is a whole different ball game. I didn't learn to shave until my freshman year in college. I went to a school that mandated that males have a face clear of a beard and mustache. It was Bible College. Before college, I shaved with a trimmer that never really gave a close shave, but it did the job.

The first time I shaved with a razor I stood in the dorm bathroom perplexed at the idea of taking a sharp object to my face and neck. An upper classman named Michael leaned over and asked me if I needed help. I am glad I was at the sink and not a urinal because if he had leaned over asking me for help there, I would have been kicked out of Bible College for starting a fight. In a juvenile manner, I said yes and he proceeded to show me how to shave with a razor. If you want to learn how to shave, visit www.therolecall.org and see a video tutorial of me showing you how to shave your mustache and beard.

Your hygiene is important. It must never be over looked. You never know what the day my bring you. You may walk by a sign that reads "Now Hiring, Walk-ins

Welcome" or you may have to be suddenly rushed to the hospital. Make sure that you are always clean.

- Health and Wellness

Before turning 23, I was lean, slim and fit. I played basketball religiously 3 times a week. It seemed like I could eat anything I wanted and never gain a pound. Even though I was active, my eating habits were horrible. I would eat a whole pack of Oreo cookies in one sitting with a warm glass of milk. If I bought chocolate chip cookie dough ice cream, the box was gone in 20 minutes. At family events, it wasn't uncommon for me to eat 2 to 3 full plates of food with soda or other highly-sweetened drinks. Little did I know that my poor eating habits would catch up to me.

After turning 23, I already had two sons. This meant that my time was cut drastically. I was no longer able to do the things that kept me active. One thing that didn't change was my eating habits. At one point I could eat a pack of Oreos and the next day work off those calories on the basketball court. Having one son was okay because he would come watch me play. When it became two, one being a newborn, it made it nearly impossible to get time in for anything else. Actually, I didn't mind not being able to play ball, all I wanted to do was spend time with my sons. Eating the way I did before my second son was born really hurt me, though.

No one told me that I had bad eating habits. From the outside looking in, I was in shape. I weighed 160 pounds soaking wet. I was often made fun of for being so skinny, but I always considered it a compliment. My weight increase didn't just come out of nowhere. I gained weight at a slow and steady pace. I would eat and eat and do nothing to stay active. All I was doing was compounding my weight. I reached a point where I didn't know what to do to lose the weight.

At 29, after a drastic change in my life, I became determined to lose the weight and get back into shape. It was then that I learned the importance of health and wellness. I was at a turning point in my life. During this time of transition, I re-evaluated every aspect of my life, including my health. I weighed 230 pounds. For several years, I was not happy with my weight, but I had gotten comfortable. I changed my eating habits, and began jogging faithfully three times a week. I felt like Forrest Gump when he said, "And from that day on, where ever I was going, I was running." I went from weighing 230 pounds to maintaining a weight between 195 and 200 pounds. I learned the balance of active living and eating right.

There is a man I know who is a big fitness guru. His name is Ronnie Heath, Jr. This is the kind of man who you wouldn't want your girlfriend to see Facebook pictures of. Muscles ripple everywhere. He is a personal trainer by trade. Fitness has become a part of his culture. Ronnie eats right and stays active and encourages others to do the same.

From youth, it is important to develop healthy eating practices. Use my story as a warning; poor eating habits will catch up to you in the long run. Put away the junk food and replace it with healthy alternatives. If you would like further resources, you can go to Ronnie's website at www.fullfocustraining.com.

- A Man Knows How To Dress For The Occasion

Doug Byrd, Jr. is a guy I know who is my age, and since he was young, his father taught him how to dress for the occasion. Here is a young man who wore the latest styles in a respectable fashion. Never once did I see him wear his pants sagging below his waist. When he attended church, he came suited up with matching shoes and socks. Doug learned this from his father. His father never looks out of place because he, too, dresses for the occasion.

I was a different story. As a teen, I wore basketball jerseys and breakaway sweat pants with shorts underneath everywhere I went - even on Sunday mornings for church. How to dress was another lesson I had to learn on my own.

Freshman year of high school I attended the year end Council For Unity banquet at a prestigious Brooklyn hall. I had enough sense not to wear basketball shorts to this event, so I decided to don a pair of jeans, a button up shirt and my fitted cap. In class one day I overheard two of the girls who would be attending discussing their outfits for the banquet and I immediately realized that I was out-classed. I went home and went into my closet to see what changes I could make to my outfit. I realized then that my wardrobe was extremely limited. I didn't even own a tie.

I asked my mother if we could go buy an outfit for the banquet. Once I told her what kind of event it was, she agreed. So, there we were in the store searching for a nice outfit for the banquet. Once we began browsing, my mother suggested I wear a suit. I replied, "For what?" I thought a nice pair of slacks and a button up was enough. Reluctantly, I wound up buying the suit, and I'm glad we did.

I showed up to the banquet where many were decked out in tuxes, suits, gowns and corsages. Man, was I out of my element. I had never been to a banquet hall for anything. In fact, I thought gratuity was a menu item till I was 19. I had no idea it referred to the tip given to a server.

The point I am making is, a man knows how to flip the script. He knows how to look his finest at a banquet and he knows how to look his "flyest" walking around in his own neighborhood.

Casual clothing ought to be presentable, too. I believe it is unacceptable for a man to sag his pants below his waist. Showing your boxers should be outlawed. I tried this fad. It was short lived. No mature man should be walking around with his pants hanging low. The purpose of a belt is to secure the pants to your waist. A man knows how to look stylish and look like a man at the same time.

● Also, do not accept a style just because everyone is wearing it. Remember, men create while boys copy. If you like a particular trend, tweak it so that it reflects your maturity. ●

I was 22 when I tied my first tie. Before that, others tied it for me and I would never loosen it. Every man should know how to tie his own tie. Clip on ties were my best friend in college. Every male was required to wear a shirt and tie to class. Although I learned to shave in college, it wasn't until my first ministry position that I learned how to tie my own tie.

Pastor Galvano smirked when I asked him to tie my tie for me. Then he said, "Are you serious, Andre?" He then proceeded to show me how. The first few times I really messed it up, but practice made perfect. I was a 22-year-old man who finally learned to tie his own tie. It may just have been a tie, but to me it was a great accomplishment.

You can also go to www.therolecall.org to see a video of me tying a tie.

- What Is True "Swagga"

My very good friend Tiffani Knowles, and editor of this book, affectionately labeled me "The Pastor With Swag." I had heard from others that I possessed a swag before I fully understood what it even meant. I wasn't sure what to make of it, but I was told that it was a good thing.

In urban terminology, "swagga" is the way one carries himself. It is made up of a man's confident walk, the way a man sounds when he talks, and what makes him distinct from others. It also defines a man's character. Many times, arrogance and swagga are used interchangeably. But, I believe there is a big difference between arrogance and "swagga," which is a healthy dose of confidence.

An arrogant man will put others down to feel better about himself. Men, by nature, are very competitive. Whether its sports, in the classroom or in the boardroom, men will compete for the upper hand. Putting another man down is what an arrogant, insecure man does. ✹ A confident man can accept the accomplishments of other men because he is content within himself.✹ Confidence is a trait that separates many men from grown boys. ✹ A man with true swagga possesses confidence, not arrogance. A man's attitude plays a big part in whether or not he possesses swag.

Swagga walks with confidence, and may even have a slight rhythm in its stride. Never does swagga waddle because his pants are hanging low. You can't exude manly confidence with your boxers showing and while walking like a duck. I remember a time when it was embarrassing for a man to show his underwear. A strong, upright, and confident walk will allow you to shine on the busiest New York City block during rush hour.

✹ Re-invent yourself. Renew your mind. Change your thinking about what a real man looks like. This is the first step you need to take to really find out what defines you. To find what makes you unique. To find what makes up your individual swag.

- Being A Man Is More Important Than Looking Like One

At some point, each of my sons has told me that they wanted to be a pastor just like me. Even some of the young boys who were a part of my youth ministry throughout the years have expressed the same sentiment. I can only assume that I was representative of what a man looked like to them. I have to say, hearing that from my sons, and the young men in my youth group, it made me feel good about my growth as a man.

My sons have seen me at my worst. There is no pretending with them. Out of everyone who has an opinion, what my sons believe about me means the most. It is easy for a man to put on a facade in front of people, but a man's children know exactly who he is. I have even seen some of my negative behaviors repeated by them, and immediately, I knew I had to change.

Although the image of a man is important, it is still only cosmetic. Until now, this chapter has been about the image of a man, but it doesn't stop with what you look like as a man. If you are going to put effort in your outward appearance, then you should put in double the effort in your inward man.

We are living in a very vain society. All is vanity. Many men seek to look more like a man than to actually be more like a man. The outside may be adorned with the facade of male adulthood, but his inside hasn't reached the fifth grade. Men ought to be what they are trying to look like. I can dress up in scrubs, a stethoscope, and a clipboard, that still doesn't make me a doctor. You can look the part of a man but still be a boy.

- Chapter Summary

Looks are fleeting. Although it is important to monitor our looks, it cannot be the measure of a man. There is a part of scripture that reads "You make his beauty melt away like a moth; Surely every man is vanity." (Psalm 39:11 KJ 2000)

The first thing a man should do is adorn his inward man with the garments that are necessary to make his character shine. This will be the indicator to himself that he is seeking to truly be a man. After this, he is more than welcome to make sure his outward appearance matches what is being done on the inside of him. Put a three-piece suit on a pig, and yet, it's still a pig.

❧ Don't just seek to look like what you think a man looks like. Seek to be a real man - a true man of action. Looking the part and being the part. ❧

Chapter 3 - Learning Beyond Experience

- Experience is a teacher

It is said that "all experience is an arch to build upon." Our experiences shape the men we become. From our character, to the way we handle situations, experience will teach us if we choose to learn from it.

Learning from experiences saves us from falling into the same trap over and over again. It reminds me of a YouTube video I saw on how to catch a monkey. This African tribesman sought to catch a monkey by placing a coconut into a small opening in a rock. The opening was wide enough for the monkey to put his hand in to grab the coconut, but once he closed his fist around the coconut the monkey was not able to get his arm out. The monkey struggled and refused to release the coconut. Even as he was approached by the tribesman, the monkey didn't relent. He just wouldn't release the coconut in an attempt to escape; therefore, he was captured.

Experience would teach a man in that same situation not to grab the coconut again. However, many men choose not to heed the lessons of experience. They fall into the same trap over and over again. Many say insanity is repeating the same actions of failure yet expecting different results. In light of the YouTube video I saw, I say when men keep falling into the same trap, it's called: "monkeying around."

"Monkeying around" is illustrated in the following statements:

"Rob, you failed another test that you didn't study for? You have to stop monkeying around."

"Vince, you got another girl pregnant? What! You didn't learn from the first girl? Stop monkeying around."

"Andre, you are playing basketball again without your ankle brace, didn't you sprain your ankle last year by not wearing it? Andre, you have to stop monkeying around."

If we do not learn from our experiences, we are no different than the monkeys that repeatedly fall into their captor's traps. The traps may be different, but the concept is the same. Learn from the experiences in your life. Do not get caught in the same traps that ensnared you in the past.

It's so important for men to learn the difference between determination and pride when it comes to experience. Determination is having a never give up attitude. Pride is having a not being upstaged attitude. Determination is a great companion as you learn from experience while pride is a killer.

The determined man will see the failures in his life experiences and adjust his actions in order to succeed. A determined man will change his approach and do what's needed to win. With a sense of humility, he may have to retreat and regroup. Once he has learned what hasn't worked, he then returns with a solution.

Pride is much different. The prideful man will not allow anyone or anything to upstage him. Instead of learning from his experiences, he will repeat the same actions because, in his mind, he knows he is right. He will not back down, and will even become ugly at times. His experience means very little to him. He will do things his way and the opposition must oblige. This is unrealistic because the opposition isn't supposed to just fall in line. He must learn the difference between determination and pride. It's like this riddle I heard while watching the *All Star Superman* movie with my sons. "What happens when the irresistible force meets the immovable object? It surrenders."

Part of breaking one's pride is heeding to the experiences of other men. Listening and learning from the experiences of others will help you learn beyond your own experiences.

- Willing to learn from others

With the many mistakes I made growing up, one thing I did consistently was learn from other men. I observed how men did things. I watched husbands interact with their wives. I studied how fathers interacted with their children. As a sentinel, I looked over the shoulders of pastors as they dealt with people and how they operated their ministries. Many of the men I watched never knew I was learning from them.

Many of the lessons I learned in my youthful observations I only started applying in the last five years. It made me a better man and an even better father. And let me make this clear; I am still learning daily and applying these lessons.

Men need to look for opportunities to learn from other men in every situation. It's what I call my "What To Dos" and my "What Not To Dos." I watch men and determine by their actions if this is something I should do, or something I should not do. Not only can we learn as we watch men do things the right way, we can also learn by watching other men do it the wrong way. That is learning what not to do.

Learning what to do is fairly easy. If what a man does produces success, then you learn from them how to do it. It's that simple. Seemingly, it's in men's nature to look at the success of other men and try to mimic what they have done so they can produce the same results. I, myself, am guilty of this. I have gained great knowledge just by watching how men do things. However, learning how not to do things is just as important.

It was a Thursday afternoon and I accepted the personal challenge of replacing my bedroom light fixture within a ceiling fan. My mother suggested that I shut off the breaker for that area of the house and I responded "Mom, I got this. All I have to do is shut the switch off and no current will go to it." Everything was going smoothly and as she watched me twist the caps over the wiring, I gleamed at her with a smugness as if to say, "See, I know what I am doing." Suddenly, sparks flew as my hands approached the red wire. I jumped off the ladder, running out of the room. My mother looked at me with this sidelong glare as if to say, "See, I told you so." This was an example of examining my situation and learning what not to do again. MAKE SURE TO SHUT THE POWER OFF IN THE SECTION OF THE HOUSE WHERE YOU ARE DOING ELECTRICAL WORK.

I almost electrocuted myself by being pigheaded.

Wise men learn from the mistakes of other men. Use the failures of other men to help you grow as a man. From other men's failures, I learned how not to speak to women, how not to interact with my mother, how not to treat a wife, how not to run a church, etc. These nuggets of knowledge I have kept with me and will continue to keep. I used their failures to maximize my success.

Heeding the advice of other men is also a huge help. This takes you diminishing your pride as a man and humbling yourself enough to learn. It's not always easy to listen to others tell you how to do things better. However, learning is our main objective; so, heeding an older man's counsel is a wise thing. No one has all the answers.

In fact, this saves you from the pain of learning only by experience. Even the advice of prideful men, men that want to tell you what to do so they feel better about themselves, you should heed, too. Ultimately, this journey is yours to walk, so humbly accept the good advice of the proud for the purposes of learning.

Be quick to listen. Develop a filter that will separate what to do and what not to do. Listen to all advice then choose whether it will benefit you or not. Just like it's important to learn in every situation, you can learn through various types of advice.

- Finding a MENtor

I have a few mentors right now. They are different depending on the characteristics they possess that I want for myself. Each one adds value to my life in some way and helps shape the man I am growing into.

Let's take Pastor Omotayo Orederu. Here is a bi-vocational pastor who works also as a lawyer. This man is deeply in love with his family. Pastor Orederu is not afraid to disclose his mistakes in hopes that they will encourage others not to walk in that same path. He also has an enormous amount of faith, passion for prayer and love for the people of God. He isn't quick to pass judgment. He is the type who listens to the whole story, then investigates the other side of the story, prays, then comes to a conclusion. He is fair and objective. These are the same attributes I desire in myself.

Then, we have Michael Peace, a youth pastor in Rochester, NY. If you were to Google the word humility, I wouldn't be surprised if Michael Peace's picture showed up. Here is a man who was the first to be signed to a major label to do Gospel rap music. He has also preached before tens of thousands in stadium events. He is a highly sought after preacher and travels extensively. Yet, he is the most approachable person I have ever met. Michael runs an urban youth outreach with hundreds of children bused in to his church every Saturday. And get this, he knows all their names. He is very accessible and has an uncanny ability to reach young people. These are all things I can learn.

My good friend Rudy Moseley is a middle school principal and pastor in Providence, RI. We attended college together. If he reads this, he would be surprised to hear that I consider him a mentor, but I do. Rudy has one of the most balanced lives I have ever seen in a man. Everything in his life he has strategized from his finances to his relationships with people. He and I used to discuss finances often. He was able to have what it appeared that he couldn't afford. And, it wasn't because of credit. Rudy has this discipline not to buy what he cannot afford. So, if he couldn't afford it, then he would save for it. In this day and age, we are more inclined to apply for credit than save for those things we really want. Rudy's foresight, among other things, is the reason I learn from him.

There are others I learn from such as Pastor Dave Watson, Pastor John Carlo, Pastor Jeremias Antonetty, Pastor Doug Byrd, Pastor Joel Hernandez, Pastor Chris Gioello, Pastor Al Cancela, Steven Sierra and Robert Young but none have made a bigger impact in my life than a man named Bob Harris.

When I first met Bob Harris, I was a little intimidated by him. Before our initial meeting, I was extremely leery of all men. My prior experiences with men outside my family were as follows: they took me under their wing to have me serve them in some capacity; I was labeled a mentee, but was used as an errand boy to advance their personal agendas. Needless to say, that was one of the major reasons for my distrust of men who were older than I was.

Bob Harris took me under his wing while I was in college. When I say he took me under his wing, it was as a duck would protect its ducklings. His main focus was to make me better and not make himself better. It didn't take much time for him to sit me down and tell me that he noticed that I didn't trust men. It was true, but I told him that he didn't know what he was talking about. He then said he didn't know my history with men but he saw potential in me and he wanted to help me reach that potential. I then asked, "What do you want with me?" He responded, "Absolutely nothing. I want you to succeed and I just want to help you get there. No strings attached." Bob was the first mentor I had who did not have his own agenda. Bob taught me how to be a mentor.

A true mentor builds up their mentees. If your mentor is consistently tearing you down, then it's time to sever the relationship. Find a mentor who has the same mindset as Bob Harris. A man that seeks to see you succeed and will help ensure your success. A good mentor desires for you to grow and eventually be better than they are.

I was once told by an older man, "Never teach everything you know because you will then become replaceable." He followed it up with, "Make sure that you are always needed so that if you ever left they would feel it." Those are not the words of a true mentor. I learned a valuable lesson when he told me that. If I leave I do want people to feel it, just as the people felt when Paul left Timothy with the church, just as the people felt when Joshua picked up the mantle of Moses to lead the people of Israel. A true mentor will teach you everything they know because they desire to leave their legacy with you. Even Jesus told His disciples, his mentees, that they would do even greater things than what He did because He wasn't going to be with them (John 14:12). That mentality may very well be the reason socialists believe that this young generation is the first generation that has not surpassed the previous one intellectually. A mentor is to teach everything they know, and allow the mentee to learn on his own.

Make sure that whoever takes you under their wing protects you. Having a mentor is more than having a man tell you what to do. A mentor is supposed to care for you. He guides you on your path and gives you the necessary tools for you to achieve success. Be wise in choosing this mentor.

Here is a checklist of what to look for:

1. A man who operates in integrity.

   His actions line up with his words. He is honest even if it hurts.

2. A man that possesses the characteristics you desire to have

   His character must exemplify the things you want to implement in your own life

3. A man who protects

   His first instinct is to protect you. He wouldn't allow anyone to speak ill of you, nor would he allow anyone to harm you in anyway.

4. A man who guides

   His example leads you in the direction that you should go. He also allows you to walk and grow, giving suggestions on how to overcome certain obstacles.

5. A man who cares

His heart is about your well-being. He will show genuine concern for you and what you care about.

- The Trust Factor

I was 10 when my mother moved us to Staten Island. I was transitioning from the fourth to the fifth grade. Here I was, the new kid in my neighborhood and in my school. A male educator at the elementary school I attended reached out to me to make me feel comfortable.

To me, he was like a grandfather figure. He would take me to local high school basketball games, bring me along as he ran errands and would even buy me gifts. I spent a lot of time in his office during recess and free time. I was happy to have a man take the time to give me what I thought was positive attention.

By the time I became a senior in high school, several articles appeared in the local papers about accusations of this male educator molesting children. I never believed it. Yeah, he would tell me he loved me and even give me a kiss on the cheek and an occasional pat on the butt. Isn't that what grandpas do?

It wasn't until I was 18 that I realized the truth. This male educator and I had lost touch throughout my high school years. I decided to invite him to my school's fashion show that I was in and he agreed. I was excited to see him because it was years since we had seen one another. I was really happy that my "grandpa" could make it. After he offered to give me a ride home, I asked if I could bring along my girlfriend and a friend of hers.

While driving to my girlfriend's house, we all exchanged great conversation. The mood was light. After he dropped the girls off, the mood changed drastically. After pulling off and driving for about a block, he pulled over and said, "Now, give me a hug." I thought nothing of it; I was giving my grandpa a hug. As I hugged him he put his hand on my chin, guided my face up to his and kissed me on my lips. I backed off him and turned my head the other way and looked out the window the rest of the ride home. I wanted to run out of the car but was afraid. My emotions ran crazy at that moment. I wanted to punch the old man right in his face.

When we got to my house, he asked for another kiss. I didn't even look at him as I jolted out of the car and slammed the door behind me. I realized that all the accusations were true. I thought back to the times he hugged me, kissed me on my cheek and patted me on my butt in disgust. This was the attempt of that sick man to gain my trust just in order to violate me.

A month after, my mother showed me an article in the paper and said, "Don't believe everything you hear."

It was another accusation of molestation surrounding this male educator. My mother knew that I cared for him as a grandfather. I then told my mother, "I am not surprised." I kept this from people because I was embarrassed. Here I am, 18 and was manipulated. Even when I was young, it was inappropriate for him to act that way toward me. He used his position to get close to a student like me in order to take advantage.

It was that incident that made it hard for me to trust older men. I protect my sons from things like that by being the man they need me to be. I show them what kind of man they should trust. And, I pity the man, or woman who tries to take advantage of my sons, or any of the young men and women I mentor. They are under my wing and I will protect them by any means necessary.

Do not just trust anyone with your well-being. Unfortunately, there are bad people out there. As a man, you have to be careful of those you let in your life. Do not be so quick to open up to everyone. Be friendly, but guard your heart. Remember that a true mentor will be a man who doesn't have his own agenda. A mentor seeks to see you succeed.

- Read Books

The fact that you are reading this book should tell you a lot about your desire to grow as a man. Many lessons can be learned through the pages of life, and many more can be learned through the pages of a book. Books can give you insight from others that will help you learn beyond your own experiences.

I learned to read at age 4. The teachers at my school treated me as a prodigy just because I was reading at a young age. While my pre-school mates were on the rooftop playground overlooking Lincoln Terrace Park in Brooklyn, I was forced to stay inside reading. By the first grade, I developed a numbness for reading.

All my life, I was a great reader. I just never comprehended what I was reading. By high school, I only read what was assigned to me. I do believe that if I had picked up a book or two or several, then that would have aided me in avoiding many a pitfall. This book is written for that very purpose, to help you avoid mistakes that young men generally make while growing up.

Throughout my years in youth ministry, I've encountered dozens of young ladies who bring books to church to read during times of fellowship. I cannot recall ever seeing a young man do the same. I only became motivated to start actively reading during my senior year in high school. Even then, I would never think to bring a book to church to read while there was a basketball gym or video games to play with my friends.

In a 2007 article I read on www.npr.org, the author Eric Weiner states, "Among avid readers surveyed by the *AP*, the typical woman read nine books in a year, compared with only five for men. Women read more than men in all categories except for history and biography." He also shares how even at young ages, girls read more than boys.

Males have less of a desire to read and it's even lower if you are a teen male. I want to congratulate you for seeking to learn beyond your own experience by picking up this book.

- Chapter Summary

It's been said that experience is the best teacher – but if you learn nothing from your experience, then it's in vain. Bottom line, learning beyond your own experience will help you avoid the mistakes that the common man will make. And, this is especially important for boys without a father. Seek to learn from other's experiences.

You cannot expect to grow as a man strictly based on your own personal experiences. Use the tips in this chapter to help you grow beyond your own experience. Use this chapter to help save you from the pitfalls that others have fallen in as they attempted to learn solely by experience. Heed the advice of the mature and never be afraid of failure. A man only fails if he stops trying to succeed.

Chapter 4 - Faith in the God of Men

- The Ultimate Example Of A Father's Love

Where is the best place a man can learn to be a father? By looking at the Father of fathers. God is the creator of all men. To wit, men were created in His image. Genesis 1:26-28 *"²⁶ Then God said, "Let Us make man in Our image, according to Our likeness; let them have dominion over the fish of the sea, over the birds of the air, and over the cattle, over all the earth and over every creeping thing that creeps on the earth." ²⁷ So God created man in His own image; in the image of God He created him; male and female He created them. ²⁸ Then God blessed them, and God said to them, "Be fruitful and multiply; fill the earth and subdue it; have dominion over the fish of the sea, over the birds of the air, and over every living thing that moves on the earth."*

The primary example of a man for a child is his father and the primary example of a man for a grown man is God. It shouldn't be a far-fetched idea to look to God as an example of what a man should be. To seek the Creator for understanding about what a man is and how to become a man, is the wisest thing a man can do.

Every created thing is created for a purpose. OxyClean was created as a solution for cleaning clothing. ShamWow was created to be a strong but gentle alternative to regular kitchen towels. A man must also know his purpose.

LOVE

God has purposed to love His creation unconditionally. With that love, He has instilled purpose into every man. Some of those purposes are universal in that every man must fulfill them; and then there are some purposes that are a little more specific. Either way, the idea that God has purposed to love us is a trait that every man must adopt. Men should possess a God-like love for people and never be ashamed of it.

At the creation of man recorded in the book of Genesis, we read that God created man and that He was well pleased. God even walked with Adam in the garden and I can only imagine the dialogue between the Creator and His creation. In one of those conversations, God explained to Adam that he was able to eat of every fruit in the garden except for the fruit of one specific tree. If he did, then he would die. Staying true to his evil, jealous nature, Satan took the form of a serpent and persuaded Adam's wife, Eve, to eat the fruit off the tree. She then persuaded Adam to follow suit.

Here is where we see the love of God manifest. I didn't realize this until I was talking with a young man who felt God set man up. At our annual youth retreat in 2005, a young man was in the back of the chapel pacing back and forth with an angry look on his face while the other teens were engaged in prayer at the altar. I noticed him and asked him to join me outside. After we left the chapel, I asked him if he was okay and he responded that he wasn't. He began to tell me how God was playing with his creation.

"Pastor Andre, if God knew we were going to fall and go to hell then how can He love us and let that happen. God set us up to fall. He's playing with us."

I paused for a minute and then responded, "When you grow up, do you want children?"

The young man said yes.

"Would you set your son up to die?" I asked.

He responded with an emphatic, "Hell no!"

"Well, if God set up man to fall then God must have set up His Son to die, too," I said. "No loving Father would ever do that."

He looked at me with a smile and said, "Pastor Andre, I see it. God loves His Son and His creation."

"Yes, and when mankind fell, God set a plan in place to redeem mankind by sending His Son Jesus to pay the price for man's shortcomings. That is true love."

The young man started to cry and joined the other teens for prayer.

God established a plan to redeem the creation He loves so much. His love was the motivation for it. God's love continued to be shown to His people several times in the pages of history.

In the time that the Jews were under Egyptian rule, God called a man to set them free from the hands of Pharaoh and to establish their own nation. During their time in the wilderness, God gave Moses a love letter in the form of the law. Many people do not consider rules and regulations an act of love, but any good parent establishes them to keep the ones they love safe from harm.

God gave Moses the Ten Commandments not to control a nation, but to establish order and institute boundaries to keep the people He loved safe. Every action has its consequences. No one is exempt from those consequences. God's motive behind His law is to show that He cares about His people.

Throughout the Bible, we see God's love for His creation and it peaked when Jesus died on the cross. God loved the world He created so much that He sent His only Son to pay the consequences for His creation's sins. That is true love. The ultimate example of love.

There is an old story about a man by the name of John Griffith who lived in Oklahoma in 1929. He lost all he had in the stock market crash. He moved to Mississippi where he took a job as bridge operator for a railroad trestle. In 1937, he was involved in a horrible accident. One day his 8-year-old son, Greg, spent the day with his Dad at work.

The boy poked around the office and asked dozens of questions – just like little boys do. The bridge was over a river and, whenever a ship came, John had to open the bridge to allow the ships to pass. The day the boy was there with his father a ship was coming, so John opened up the draw bridge.

After a moment or two, he realized his son wasn't in the office and as he looked around, to his horror, John saw his son climbing around on the gears of the draw bridge. He hurried outside to rescue his son but just then he heard a fast approaching passenger train, the Memphis Express, filled with 400 people. He yelled to his son but the noise of the now clearing ship and the oncoming train made it impossible for the boy to hear him. All of a sudden John Griffith realized his horrible dilemma. If he took the time to rescue his son the train would crash killing all aboard, but if he closed the bridge, the boy would be crushed in the gears.

John would sacrifice his son. He made the horrible decision, pulled the lever and closed the bridge. It is said, as the train went by, John could see the faces of the passengers, some reading, some even waving, all of them oblivious to the sacrifice that had just been made for them. (Taken from www.thesource4ym.com)

This mirrors God's love for us. God's example of a loving father is to be emulated. The true fact is that we will never possess the amount of love for our own children that God has for us; however, we can mimic what we learn from God.

- God's Idea And Role Of Manhood

The only place I can turn to is the Bible for this information. Many consider the Bible to be out of date, but despite the time in which the Scriptures were written, the principles found in the Bible can be used to bring clarity to the role of a man.

Every piece in a machine has its role to play and men are no different. Men need to understand how to play the role they have been given. Communities crumble because men choose not to take their rightful place in society. This causes an imbalance. Women then must pick up the role of a man to compensate for men's lack. This causes the scales to tip and, frankly, it's partly the man's fault.

To return things to a healthy balance, we must apply the principles found in the Bible. Even if you are not a Christian, the Bible will help you learn the role you ought to play in society.

Protector

God has put a protective instinct in every man. Men will protect and defend people and things that are closest to them. From family to friends to objects, a man will seek to ensure the safety of the people and things he loves.

Jesus also said that there is no greater love than one who gives their lives for a friend. [John 15:13] This is shown to us in the Bible when we read that husbands are to love their wives even as Christ loves His church and gave His life for her. [Ephesians 5:25]

Teacher

The first lesson a child learns is not in the classroom. It's in the home. Men have the charge to teach by word and by example. Children will watch and learn some of life's early lessons by watching the adults living in the home. A man must exemplify the lessons he wishes to teach. Not just in the home, but in his community, too.

Men ought to pass on wisdom and knowledge to the generation behind him. In my experience, most men desire authority, but with that authority he must begin to teach righteously. He must teach lessons that will improve the overall society in which he lives.

Men were charged in the Bible to teach the children God's commandments and to sit and discuss them [Deuteronomy 6:7] We can also read in the Bible that if we train up a child in the way they should go, when they grow up, those lessons will not leave them [Proverbs 22:6]

Wise

Many men profess to be wise based on their experiences. Experience alone won't qualify you as a wise man. It's the understanding of your experiences. As I said in chapter 3, not learning from your experiences makes you as wise as a monkey.

Wisdom begins with God so every man ought to seek God for it. The book of Proverbs mentions wisdom in 51 verses and, in 67 verses, the word wise is mentioned. Reading Proverbs will help you understand that true wisdom is Godly wisdom.

"making your ear attentive to wisdom and inclining your heart to understanding" [Proverbs 2:2]

Slow To Wrath

Anger can be a very ugly thing. The mere fact is that at some point in every man's life he is faced with a situation that angers him, but a man should not allow that anger to overtake him. As a man, managing your anger is important. When something is done that angers you, make sure not to display your wrath, but reserve the wrath for the One who can judge righteously.

The Bible says that the wrath of man does not produce the righteousness of God [James 1:20] Let wrath stay in its rightful place, and that is with God. Every action has its consequences. Let us not be quick to be angry but instead listen and understand the offender.

Know this, my beloved brothers: let every person be quick to hear, slow to speak, slow to anger [James 1:19]

Community-minded

Let me first differentiate between being community-minded and being politically-minded. A man who is community-minded seeks to improve his neighborhood rather than be seen, while the man who is political selfishly improves his neighborhood for personal gain.

Communities need more men that are willing to improve their neighborhoods. Just recently, an 18-month-old was shot in a building complex less than a mile from my home. Men should seek to start positive movements in their communities to see that things like this don't happen. All throughout the Bible, we see examples of men who loved their communities -- from Moses, to Joshua, to David, to Daniel to Jesus.

Use this scripture as a guide for how men ought to uphold justice in their communities:

"⁹ Let love be genuine. Abhor what is evil; hold fast to what is good. ¹⁰ Love one another with brotherly affection. Outdo one another in showing honor. ¹¹ Do not be slothful in zeal, be fervent in spirit, serve the Lord. ¹² Rejoice in hope, be patient in tribulation, be constant in prayer. ¹³ Contribute to the needs of the saints and seek to show hospitality.

¹⁴ Bless those who persecute you; bless and do not curse them. ¹⁵ Rejoice with those who rejoice, weep with those who weep. ¹⁶ Live in harmony with one another. Do not be haughty, but associate with the lowly. Never be wise in your own sight.

¹⁷ Repay no one evil for evil, but give thought to do what is honorable in the sight of all. ¹⁸ If possible, so far as it depends on you, live peaceably with all. ¹⁹ Beloved, never avenge yourselves, but leave it[c] to the wrath of God, for it is written, "Vengeance is mine, I will repay, says the Lord." ²⁰ To the contrary, "if your enemy is hungry, feed him; if he is thirsty, give him something to drink; for by so doing you will heap burning coals on his head." ²¹ Do not be overcome by evil, but overcome evil with good." [Romans 12:9-21]

That is just the tip of the iceberg. There is much a man can learn about being a man from reading the pages of Scripture. As I said, even if you do not consider yourself religious, many of the principles are universal and plainly -- just make sense.

- Examples Of Manhood In The Bible

From Genesis to Revelation, we can read about the examples of men in history. Some of those examples we can follow and some we should not. Yes, even in the Bible you will see some of men's failures, causing tragic consequences.

Let's take the very first man for instance. In the book of Genesis we read about how Adam was given the task to name all the creatures on the earth and to tend to the Garden of Eden. God bestowed on Adam a great *responsibility*.

After the naming of all the animals, God made woman from Adam's rib. He finally had a helper who was comparable to him to help him tend to the Garden. Now, let's go back to man's first moment of failure. The one boundary that was established for Adam was for him not to eat from the tree of good and evil and Adam crossed it. Please take note that the boundary was given to Adam, not Eve. Eve is not to blame for man's failure. It was Adam's fault because God told Adam not to eat of the tree even before Eve was created.

Also, in Genesis, we read about a man called Abraham. Here is a man who was so obedient to God that he was willing to sacrifice his promised son. God instructed Abraham to sacrifice his son to test Abraham's

obedience. God promised Isaac to Abraham in his old age, and God finally delivered him, only to tell Abraham to give him back. But prior to that, Abraham failed in many areas.

Abraham lied to kings. Abraham had to part ways with his nephew because of family differences. Instead of trusting God, he allowed his wife to convince him to take his maid servant and impregnate her so that they could have a child. All these failures led Abraham to the point of obedience, to the point where he was willing to sacrifice his son.

Now let me make this perfectly clear, THAT WAS A ONE TIME OCCURENCE. God will not expect you to sacrifice your own children, just as God really didn't want Abraham to. He was testing Abraham and he passed. You do not ever have to worry about passing that test, because Abraham is the only man and will be the only man that has or will ever take that test. What God told Abraham to do is different from the story of the man from Oklahoma who chose to save the lives of the train passengers. The father made a choice to save them and wasn't commanded to sacrifice his son for them.

You can also read about Moses in the book of Exodus. He was called by God to lead the Israelites out of Egyptian slavery. Moses reluctantly heeded God's call and became a **leader** to a nation. Through him, many signs and wonders were performed to show the omnipotence of God. In result, Pharaoh had no choice but to release the Israelites.

Moses also heeded the advice of his elders. Moses became overwhelmed and accepted his father-in-law's advice to appoint leaders under him that would help with the affairs of the people. In turn, organization and governmental structure became established, even to a people who did not yet possess a land.

Moses was also very emotional, causing him to fail. In his anger, he disobeyed God. In the book of Numbers, you can read about how God directed Moses to speak to a rock for water to spring out. Instead, because of his frustration with the people and his unbelief, Moses struck the rock with his rod and water came springing out. This resulted in Moses not being able to enter into the Promised Land when they finally reached it.

Let's go into the book of Judges as I tell you about Samson. Samson was known for taking down a lion with his bare hands and for killing a thousand men with a jaw bone of a donkey in defense of his people. Samson possessed great **strength**.

Samson's failure came by way of his lust for a woman. Samson trusted a harlot who was also a spy to the enemy of his people. After revealing to her the secret to his strength, the harlot told his enemies the secret and they were able to capture him.

Now let's look at the mighty King David. You can read about King David in 1 Samuel. King David was acknowledged as a man after God's own heart. David was a noted warrior but even above that David loved to **worship** God. David was one of the authors of the book of Psalms, a poetic book of worship and prayers found in the Bible. David was also an accomplished musician.

Even King David wasn't perfect. One night, King David spotted a woman bathing while he was walking on his roof. He noticed that she was beautiful and sent his servants to inquire about her. He knew the woman was married and that her husband was in battle, the very battle where King David should have been. He slept with her anyway and when he found out she was pregnant, David set up her husband to die in battle.

There is only one man who did everything except fail and that was Jesus Christ.

- Jesus: The Ultimate Example Of Manhood

You cannot get any manlier than Jesus Christ. He was the ultimate example of what manhood is all about. Many people believe various things about Jesus, but the one thing that all can agree on was that He was a Great Man. His teachings changed the world forever. His example started a movement that has been matched by none. Jesus is the Man.

All throughout the Gospels (Matthew, Mark, Luke & John), we can read up on the many things he did as a man. I can write a book on that alone, and I just might do that after this.

Jesus stood for what He was most passionate about - God and God's people. Even if you read the smallest morsel of any of the Gospels, you will see that He stood true to what He represented. As He walked teaching God's words and principles, He also was an example to all who saw Him. Jesus wasn't just talking, He was living.

Not even the devil himself could deter Jesus from His mission. Beyond being tempted in every way, Jesus was also betrayed by the people He loved and came to Earth for. Despite that betrayal, Jesus still went to the cross, suffering the consequences for the wrongs He didn't commit so that we wouldn't have to undergo the same penalty. Jesus is all the things the greatest men in the world were, plus more. Reading about His life here on earth will help us understand the model of what a true man should be. Not just to himself, but to his spouse, children, family, and community.

- Men In The Church

When I was a child, I would occasionally attend church with my godmother in Brooklyn. The one thing that always stood out to me was the fact that there were more women in the church than there were men. This church was a soulful Baptist church where the women were professional clappers. They were able to make their two hands sound like a full percussion band. I would sit in fascination when I visited that church.

The only men I would see consistently whenever I did go to church with her were the men behind the pulpit. Maybe because it's Sunday and it's NFL season, I would think. Should that be an excuse for a man not to accompany his family, or better yet, lead his family to a church service? Not at all.

Men have the esteemed call to be the spiritual head of their families. When we look at church membership today, men are outnumbered by the women in almost every congregation, not just in America but around the world. God called the men to lead their families in the ways of God. The best example to a son on how to be a spiritual man is the example of his father. Women have had to pick up a mantle left by the man as the spiritual head of the home.

The man should be leading the family to church, not the woman. We read in the early chapters of Deuteronomy in the Bible that God mentions to Moses to instruct the men to diligently teach their children and grandchildren about God's ways. To the women that will be reading this next statement, it's not that I'm being a sexist or a bigot, I am simply encouraging men to take their rightful place at the head of their families. Men, you are called to be the head of your home. You are not a ruler of your home, but a watchman and teacher of those in your home. It's not the woman's role to spiritually rear up your children. That is your job. Step up and Man up. Take your place in your home NOW.

- What Is Salvation

A man cannot guide his family spiritually if he isn't first equipped to walk in that path. Salvation isn't an extremely hard concept to grasp; in fact, it is fairly easy and what better way to explain it than letting the Word of God give the explanation!

For Moses writes that the law's way of making a person right with God requires obedience to all of its commands. But faith's way of getting right with God says, "Don't say in your heart, 'Who will go up to heaven' (to bring Christ down to earth). And don't say, 'Who will go down to the place of the dead' (to bring

Christ back to life again)." In fact, it says, "The message is very close at hand; it is on your lips and in your heart."

And that message is the very message about faith that we preach: If you confess with your mouth that Jesus is Lord and believe in your heart that God raised him from the dead, you will be saved. For it is by believing in your heart that you are made right with God, and it is by confessing with your mouth that you are saved. As the Scriptures tell us, "Anyone who trusts in him will never be disgraced." Jews and Gentiles are the same in this respect. They have the same Lord who gives generously to all who call on him. For "everyone who calls on the name of the LORD will be saved."

Romans 10:5-13 (NLT)

- Chapter Summary

Having faith in the God of men is an essential part of growing as a man. Remember that things that are created usually come with an operating manual. As for men, our operating manual is the Bible.

When I buy furniture that I have to assemble, I always read the manual to make sure that I build it properly. The same concept goes for men. For men to ensure that they are growing properly, seeking the creator of man and His manual is key to growing as a man.

And to top it all off, God sent His Son Jesus to be the ultimate example of a man. Even if you do not want to be a Christian, Jesus' examples and the principles found in the Bible will help you grow as a man. However, my hope is that you do receive the joy and liberty that come with Salvation.

Chapter 5 - A Strong Will and a Soft Heart

- Strength In A Man's Will

Oxymoron: a combination of <u>contradictory</u> or incongruous words. As strange as it seems, men must be oxymorons from time to time. In the case of having a strong will and a soft heart, this is the classic example. One of the most negative traits found in men can be one of the most useful traits if applied properly. This trait is most commonly known as a man's stubbornness.

Coincidently, the word ox is found in the prefix of oxymoron. The simile "as stubborn as an ox" is derived from an ox's nature to do what it wants when it wants to do it. Once an ox wills itself to do something or not to do something, very little can be done to convince it otherwise.

Young men need to develop an ox-like stubbornness - a strong will. A man's will is a very powerful thing. A man can accomplish many things once he puts his mind to it.

Take me for example. Statistics say I should have become an absentee father just as my father was. Regardless of the odds against me, I determined in myself never to turn my back on my children. I was tested when it came to a grueling battle to gain physical custody of my three sons. However, I refused to be a father who wasn't there for my children every day for the rest of my life.

I set out to be the father to my children that I never had. I am not a perfect father by any means, but I promised to be the best father I could be to my sons. I will myself every day to be that father.

My younger brother Anton is another example. I couldn't ask for a better younger brother. He has been such a support to my children and I. I mention him when I encourage young men who must strengthen their resolve to do better in school.

From Anton's time in junior high school and even toward the beginning of his high school years, he was a subpar student. He wasn't a bad kid. He just was not focused on his studies. In fact, a day after I moved back to Staten Island after returning from Bible college and living in Rochester, NY, I caught him cutting school at a park across the street from the house of a friend of mine. He tried to dodge me so I wouldn't spot him, but his afro and stocky frame made him hard to miss.

His junior year in high school was Anton's turning point. He literally willed himself to do better in school. He stopped getting into trouble, began associating himself with more scholastic-minded peers, he - an avid video gamer - even limited his Xbox and PlayStation 2 time to focus on his studies.

The will to do well in school followed Anton to college where he excelled in his field of study. Anton has now begun an illustrious career as a computer tech associate for one of the country's top companies.

A man must have a will to achieve the goals he sets out for himself. Your will power can cause you to stand in the midst of failure and persevere beyond it to gain success. You have to be a fighter, never accepting defeat as an option.

This same will power will assist you in resisting daily temptations that bombard you. It will assist you in resisting addictions. And when the pressure is too much and you feel like you do not have the strength of will to fight, God will always provide that help.

In chapter 2, I told you about my will to lose weight. Every year on January 1, from 2004 to 2010, I would resolve to get in shape. I purchased a treadmill and a Bowflex because I wanted to get ripped. And every year on or about January 14, I would forget that resolution and resort back to eating a whole pack of Double Stuffed Oreos with a glass of warm milk.

In 2010, I finally willed myself to lose the weight and to get in shape. Fifty-five pounds were lost because I willed myself to lose the weight. That same will power, if you tap into, will help you achieve any goal you set out for yourself.

- Strength In Submission to God's Will

Some challenges are extremely difficult to face. The will of man may be strong but there may come a time in your life where you may be ready to tap out. I can guarantee it. It happens to every man. A man may reach a point in his life where he is ready to give up the fight. For many of you, it was the very reason your father left, forcing you to learn how to become a man for yourself.

I have willed myself to succeed within the face of various oppositions. Severe opposition has come from loved ones, family, so-called friends and even the very men that were set over me as mentors. I have felt really alone many days. Often, I have felt my will fading away. In those rough times, I leaned on God and prayed to Him to pull me through.

I have heard men say that people use God as a crutch and, the truth is, that they are right. I am a man that uses God as a crutch all the time. Not only is God my crutch when I am broken, He's also my Anchor so I stay grounded.

There will come a time where you will feel your will crumbling. Know that it isn't cowardly to use God as a crutch when you do not have the strength to press on. As strong as your will power is, allowing God to enhance it by your submission to His will can only enable you to become stronger.

God has a plan for every man. Some of those plans are universal for every man to follow such as being a provider for his family, fleeing from youthful lusts, etc. However, God has more specific plans for individual men. The plan and vision that you have in your heart to better yourself right now comes from God. It is His will for you as an individual man.

When God gives a man a plan and a vision, God also equips him with the will power to see it through. God will never put more on you than you can handle.

Submission to God also saves men from getting into unnecessary trouble. Every bad thing comes from the enemy (the devil) and submission to the will of God enables you to resist the enemy. The Bible says in James 4:7, *"Submit yourselves therefore to God. Resist the devil, and he will flee from you."* Your will power at times will not be enough to get you through. So, make sure to tap into God's reserve, which is only found as you submit to Him.

Submission to God is a sure fire way of success in life. When you submit to God, your troubles will flee from you.

- Strength In Compassion

This next portion is for all the young men who have been fooled into thinking that compassion is a sign of weakness. I'd like to refute that wholeheartedly. Compassion means you have the strength to look out not only for yourself, but for others. Any man who shows compassion in any situation displays a great level of strength because strength isn't just about imposing your will on another. No, that's being a bully. The man who is truly strong is able to offer his strength to others and be a help to them. Unfortunately, this idea hasn't achieved popularity in many arenas of life.

In Their School

Bullies tend to run the schools they attend. Whether she is a cheerleader, he is captain of the football team or a knuckleheaded youth who intimidates his peers, these young persons tend to set the social culture of the schools they attend.

If a student trips and falls and drops all their books as they are rushing through the hallways, the surrounding students are more likely to laugh. Compassion says a student should have the strength to make sure the student that fell is okay and then help them pick up their books.

In school, I was always fairly popular. I was the type of student who knew everyone, from the athletes to the mathletes. I got along with everyone and it allowed me to obtain favor.

The teachers and other faculty even took notice and praised me for it. Here I am, a young, fatherless, Black-Hispanic American from one of the roughest neighborhoods in NYC going to school showing compassion to everyone. I went against the grain as a young man growing up in the "hood."

I obtained favor in the eyes of the adults in my life because of my compassion. As I was walking through Costco recently, Mr. Marotta, the principal of the high school I attended spotted me. He stopped me and told me he remembered how nice a student I was, always looking out for my peers. This was surprising to me because my high school had a student body of about 4,000 students.

Another positive thing about me expressing compassion was that it would rub off on others. I encouraged others to demonstrate compassion. It was sort of like, "If Andre – as cool as he is - is nice to this guy, then maybe we should try being nice, too." I wasn't always successful in getting them to practice compassion all the time, but I never stopped trying.

In Their Neighborhood

The urban jungles are where young men are trained to be heartless and ruthless. The name of the game for urban men is survival. It seems there is no room for compassion in the "hood." Young men must appear hard and unfeeling. They believe that compassion is the equivalent to being soft. The harder a young man is, the safer he is. My nature is the complete antithesis.

I grew up on Mariners Harbor in Staten Island, NY in a house right across the street from the city's housing projects. I survived, not by being hard, but by being the opposite. I had a loving heart toward people. I didn't try to be hard because I wasn't. I later realized that the harder you try to be hard, the more you are tested to see how hard you really are.

One night at about 11:30 p.m., my doorbell rang. And as I looked outside, there were about nine guys from the neighborhood yelling for me to come outside. I knew them all because we played ball at the local park together. My mother was extremely agitated by the whole thing and refused to let me go outside. Even I was afraid, but I went outside to see what they wanted.

I went outside and the guy that rang my door was standing in front of me with a gun on his hip. He began to tell me that a close friend of mine was running his mouth and that he was ready to do him in. But, he said he respected me because I was cool and real and didn't want to do anything that would disrespect me. I was able to talk him out of it.

He considered me real, not because of how hard I was but because I never tried to be something I wasn't. I sought peace in every situation and showed compassion to the people in my neighborhood. I didn't need to be hard to survive in the hood. I just needed to be myself.

My compassionate spirit also brought me favor with the parents in my neighborhood. I can't begin to count how many mothers and fathers wanted me to date their daughters. I was the nice boy on the block. I carried groceries, opened gates and doors, even helped with outdoor chores. I was the boy that parents didn't mind their children hanging out with.

Compassion is the kind of strength that has been discounted in the rearing up of young men for some time. You are not "soft" for showing kindness to another person. It is what separates us from animals – our ability to empathize.

Survival in the urban jungle usually equates to "kill or be killed." Pastor Cherry, pastor of From The Heart Church in Maryland, said in a service I watched on TV one Sunday morning that young males in urban communities are killing themselves. They are a new kind of endangered species. He went on to say that every other endangered species is removed from their environment and put in a safe place to be preserved. I believe this self-genocide can be attributed to weak men who downplay compassion as a legitimate form of strength.

Change your outlook on compassion. Compassion is raw strength. This is the type of strength that also strengthens others around you. Be strong, young man. Be compassionate.

- A Soft Heart Beats Firmly

The heart pumps life throughout the body. Without that internal reservoir we would all cease to exist. In the same way, a soft heart pumps life throughout our communities. We need men who aren't afraid to be tender-hearted.

Many communities, specifically urban communities, fail to express a genuine heart for the neighborhoods they reside in. In my experience, men are more focused on getting than giving back to their communities. Drug dealers take from their communities so they can fill their pockets. The younger men in many urban communities stand idly by as drug dealers destroy their hoods all while amassing wealth. These young men have no choice to look up to these upwardly mobile figures, and eventually follow in the older drug dealers' footsteps.

The drug dealer analogy was an extreme one; however, there are still men who care very little for their communities even though they can be upstanding, law-abiding citizens. These types of men go to work, come home and, as they commute from home to work, and vice versa, they put up side blinders ignoring the needs of their neighborhoods. No wonder our young men lack a love for their communities.

It takes great strength for a man to care for his community. A man who tears down his neighborhood doesn't show strength but weakness, a low self-worth. A man tears down his community because he wants others to feel lower than him.

A man with a soft heart expresses strength by spreading positivity to his community. He possesses an amazing reservoir of power. This man desires to see others achieve more than he could ever accomplish. A man with a soft heart has no other motives other than to show compassion by giving of himself to others.

Growing up I have had the honor of observing both these types of men in action. Unfortunately, the men with the soft heart are a minority. Men like Gerry Mosely who trains youth in the fundamentals of basketball, the late Ron Bolden who was instrumental in taking many of the young men in my neighborhood to see the world outside our tiny section of Staten Island, Tyrone Landrum who was respected in my neighborhood for looking out for young men, and Rev. Lawrence Hallahan who was a white man way outside his element who served teens in urban communities, these are to name a few. None of these men were perfect but their strength shined through in the legacy they left behind. Until this day, their strength lives on as I try to reach out to young men everywhere. These men had soft hearts that beat firmly.

- Humility Does Not Mean Weak

Growing up, I was a good basketball player. I certainly wasn't the best but I knew the game well enough to play my role and play it well. It was 1990 while in the fifth grade that I first fell in love with the fame. Mr. Bruno, my fifth grade gym teacher drew out a talent in me that I never thought I had and from then on I loved the game of basketball. I still remember going from being the last one picked or not being picked at all to being the first one everyone wanted on their team.

Basketball is one sport that is characterized by pride. Talking trash, putting the opponent down, even tearing down teammates for you to shine is something I am way too used to. Still, I never fit the bill. I was never the trash-talking type; in fact, I was the player that let my game talk for me. You can say that my silence was my hustle because I just never really saw the need to hype myself up.

While my opponents trash-talked, I usually shut them up by letting my game speak. I didn't always win but even in my losses, my point came across loud and clear. They were able to see my strength in my humility.

In my opinion, for a man to boast in himself, it screams low self-esteem. Self-confidence is silent. No words are necessary. You cannot tell people how great you are. Show them first. At the same time, your greatness has to be expressed without putting people down.

If a man tears another down as he boasts about himself, he is really saying "I am not that great. I just want you to believe I am greater than you." On the contrary, a man with humility is self aware and doesn't consider himself better than anyone. Humility doesn't have to tear another person down to lift itself up; in fact, humility will make another feel much better about himself.

- Chapter summary

Realize the strength in having a soft heart while balancing a strong will. We, as men, are stronger than we realize. God gave us free will and He also gave us the strength to choose right. You are strong and, with God's help, and in following His will, you will never fall.

Don't be afraid to express compassion and humility. There is tremendous strength in that. I plead with you not to disconnect your emotions and purge the very thing that makes you strong. If you dismiss compassion and humility then you become numb and weak. Be strong and let your heart be soft.

Chapter 6 - Act on Your Word

- What is a man of Integrity

One day, I went out and asked a couple of young men to tell me the definition of integrity; sadly, the majority of the young men I asked had no clue what integrity was even though they had heard the word before. I also asked some young women that same question; many of them offered similar responses -- honesty.

Integrity is a huge part of being a real man. Integrity: a firm adherence to a code of especially moral and ethical or artistic value. Thanks to good ole Webster for furnishing such a precise definition. The dilemma: how can a young man learn this without a man to show him? Or how can a young man learn this when his "deadbeat" father isn't at all an example of this?

It seems the average adult male will seek to get ahead in life by any means necessary, even at the expense of being dishonest. This is not what a man ought to do. It simply doesn't show good character. Sadly, the majority of the examples of men who seem successful boast behaviors that have advanced them by dishonest means.

Many business men use cutthroat tactics to gain position or trump a competitor. Musicians make music by lying about their lifestyles. Politicians defame the character of their opponents so they can get the votes. It seems that the example of a man of integrity is nonexistent.

Even I have fallen short in this area time and time again. A couple of years ago, I realized I had a talent for editing video and decided to try my hand at being a wedding videographer. I had the opportunity to do several weddings and the end products were great.

The last two weddings I got contracted to do happened at a point in my life that was very trying for me. On top of that, the computer I used for editing the videos crashed on me. For months, I tried to fix the problem and then months turned into years. It finally got to the point where I wasn't able to fix the problem and was unable to deliver the project they paid for, resulting in the couples' disappointment.

The fact that I wasn't able to deliver on my word tore me up inside. My integrity was compromised in their eyes. I wasn't the man I said I was. I made a promise and the promise fell through. One thing that every man should desire is for a reputation of being a man of integrity.

In all the lessons I have learned about being a man, integrity is one that directly affects another's opinion of who you really are.

- The value of a man's word

This folktale is one that has been told for ages and will be told for ages to come. A young shepherd boy, while watching sheep, shouts "Wolf!" He causes other shepherds to run, ready to defend the sheep from the ravenous wolf they thought was attacking the flock. Realizing there was no wolf, the men walk off and went about their business.

A second time, the shepherd boy shouts "Wolf!" and again the other shepherds come running ready to defend the flock of sheep. This time, they realize that the shepherd boy was playing a joke on them and they walk off, warning him that he shouldn't lie because "next time people will not believe you." A third time, the shepherd boy shouts "Wolf!" but this time, no one responded. No one came to his rescue as a vicious wolf grabs a sheep from the flock.

Frantic, he ran screaming for help but no one would believe him because his word was - at this point – worthless.

Words have no value to the person who doesn't value his words. A man must value what he says before anyone else can value his words. Mind what you say. Do not speak words just to say them. Think about what you say first, and then evaluate its importance. After you realize what you have to say has any worth, then say it.

In a study done by researchers at the University of Arizona in 2007, on average, men and women utter about the same amount of words per day. The study revealed that women, on average, say about 16,215 words a day while men say 15,669.

The issue isn't how many words are being spoken, but the quality of the words you say. In all the years of my life, observing both men and women, I have found that speech content is different among the male and female gender. To be frank, neither gender has an edge over the other when it comes to valuing the words they speak.

It's no secret that women's speech, in general, tends to be filled with gossip. However, men tend to lie, mislead and carry on conversations that are lewd. Although I can offer nuggets about the value of a woman's word, this book is dedicated to helping my sons and other young men who are reading it.

A man's word is worth more than any precious metal or jewel. Words of wisdom are usually termed nuggets or jewels because of their worth. You can have all the money in the world, but if your words are of no value, then who you are is of no value.

As men, we must transition our thinking from placing value on things like money and sex to placing value on our words. We must choose our words wisely so that we may add value to others. Men desire to be heard when they say something; however, there is no one on the earth who will want to hear what you have to say if it doesn't have value. All the money in the world will not change that.

To fathers, if you do not keep your word to your children, your word will begin to diminish in its value, eventually becoming worthless to them. Your direction and your advice, as sound as it may be, will become meaningless. Telling them that they need to do better in school after you have repeatedly fallen back on your promises to spend time with them, or to buy them something they need, will not be received.

Young men, the words you speak ought to have value. Here are some tips to make your words solid gold:

1. Tell the truth
   Even if you risk getting in trouble, be honest about it.
2. Act on your word
   If you say something, then you must do it. Keep promises or don't make them.
3. Choose your words wisely
   Make sure that if you have something to say that it's worth saying. Do not just speak to hear the sound of your voice. Speak when it's time to say something.
4. Never gossip
   Generally, men aren't known to be gossipers, but it does happen. If what you hear has nothing to do with you, then you have no reason to spread it to others.
5. Do not try to force others to hear your opinion
   You have to know that your words are worth listening to. If you are speaking to someone

who does not want to listen, then keep it moving.

6. Listen, then carefully respond

   In a discussion or argument, before you share your views or opinions, make sure the other party has completely expressed themselves first. Understand their point of view first, then share what you have to say. Listening and understanding is a huge part of adding value to your words. If you appear to be closed-minded, your words will be voided to others.

- Power in the tongue

Proverbs 18:21 says *"Death and life are in the power of the tongue."* This isn't in reference to the actual body part but rather to what we use the body part to do. This has to do with your language and your words. What you say has the power to bring death or give life. It's simple. What you say has tremendous power.

The saying "sticks and stones may break my bones but words will never hurt" is so far from the truth. Words hurt more because they stick to who you are and how you feel about yourself. Hit me with a stick, my wounds will heal. Hurt me with your words and those words will bruise forever. With that knowledge, a man is to make sure his speech is salted with positivity that will give life and not bring death.

In war, it's not the men on the front lines with rifles and grenades controlling the battle. It's the men giving the orders. The President of the United States has all the power in the world and doesn't have to pick up a weapon to wield it. All he has to do is say it. At the end of 2011, President Barack Obama called an end to the war in Iraq from the Oval Office simply by saying, "It's over. Pull the troops out." In that same manner, you as a man must use your words to wield your power.

Some men believe that if they are able to beat a man down, then they possess power. On the contrary, the real victor in a fight is the one who is able to get the other to understand their side. Herein lies the true evidence of the power of the tongue. A fist to my face will not allow me to see your point of view; in fact, it may not allow me see at all because of a possible swollen eye. The Bible says that a soft answer turns away wrath but harsh words stir up anger. Truer words there never were.

As a man, your duty in society is to spread seed that would give life. Speak life in to people in your community. Encouraging words will make the suicidal introvert help see that he is important and begin to value his life. Encouraging words can help a young man think twice about fighting. Encouraging words can help a young man believe he can achieve anything he sets his heart and mind to. Spread the seeds of positive speech, and watch life grow around you.

Men have to utilize the power of language more often. As a young man learns "what to say," "how to say it" and "to whom to say it" is also important. I grew up in an urban neighborhood, lived with a Trinidadian grandmother who always spoke proper English, went to a high school where the majority of the students were Caucasian and had friends of all nationalities. I am one person who knows how to communicate.

I would consider myself a chameleon, linguistically speaking. I am able to speak to young people in terms they understand and I can speak to a board room of industry professionals so that they can understand. This doesn't mean you are a sell out. It makes you versatile. It's you using the power of the tongue to get ahead. This is how you breathe life into your manhood.

Expecting everyone to cater to your style of speech is unrealistic and makes you an immature man. Going through life speaking slang will only cripple you. Do not use your favorite rap artist as an example. They are a huge part of the "Dumbing of the American Teenager," which is the title of one of the books I am writing presently. Get a dictionary and learn the definitions of new words. Use them in their proper context. Grow in your use of vocabulary. This will not only impress your listeners but it will give you greater self-confidence.

- Power in silence

Silence is the most valuable weapon a man has if he uses it properly. It will save you from situations where you have to go back on your words.

Let's say you are talking with someone who is bragging about the amount of girls he has been with, and you choose to lie and say you have been with more. What if he says, "Prove it." Now there's pressure for you to try to back up a lie. If you remain silent, it will save you from embarrassment.

A man knows when to speak, and what to say when needed. Boys speak nonsense and men speak what makes sense. Now, men may pepper their dialogue with topics that seem boyish at times, but even in those conversations, a good knowledge base of the topic is expected. Sports, movies, cars, video games and - dare I say it - women.

Men speak about what they know. If you do not know about a particular topic that is being discussed, stay silent and learn. You will gain the power of knowledge - learning something you didn't know. If you want to prove you know everything and talk about a topic you know nothing about, you will only end up sounding like an idiot. In this arena, your best and only option is to stay silent.

This goes back to valuing your words. Talking about what you have little to no knowledge of only devalues your word. If you have no knowledge of a particular topic of conversation, your silence is more valuable to you than your words. As I said, put yourself in a position to learn something new. After you have gained knowledge, then you are free to engage in meaningful conversation, instead of the alternative -- sounding foolish.

Silence is also a key to conflict resolution. Silence doesn't always equate to passivity. Silence is a tool of strategy. You may be surprised how silence can diffuse a disagreement. People who yell when they argue will only yell if someone is yelling back. If you are being yelled at, just sit and listen. It works like magic. Watch the aggressor's volume lower and their attitude change. Resistance only brings more resistance. Silence will allow you to be in control of the situation. It will help you keep your head, as long as you do not let what is being said affect you. This is particularly true concerning relationships. We will address this more in detail in Chapter 7 when I tell you about appreciating a woMan.

Learn how to use your tongue to bring life to every situation. This is a mark of a man with true character.

- The difference between say-ers and do-ers

This is fun for me to write about. Here is where I get to briefly describe my opinion about the difference between men who run their mouths and men who run with their mouths. I am going to be so judgmental in this portion. So, please excuse my irreverence in advance.

This book is about manhood and one of the things men need to be able to do is receive harsh criticism from time to time. If you are offended, then suck it up, listen to the words you are reading right now and make a change.

Say-ers are lazy, do-ers are not. Talk all you want. If you do not move on your word, you are nothing but a lazy nothing. It takes zero effort to say what you want to see done. Talking all you want about doing something and not getting it done makes you unreliable. That means you cannot be counted on. Do-ers put forth the effort. They rise up, take the bull by its horns and will wrestle it to the ground by any means necessary.

Say-ers are weak, do-ers are not. Yes, I am telling you that if you talk a good talk and do not follow through, then you are a weak excuse for a man. We all have been there, but real men do not stay there. Strength is found in the action after what is said. Talking and not doing is only a form of weakness. That is why there are so many weak fathers out there. They talk, make promises and rarely follow through on their word. Being vocal doesn't make you strong, in fact, it can prove how weak you really are if you do not follow through.

Say-ers are cowards, do-ers are not. This reminds me of a YouTube video I saw recently where a little Pug dog was at the top of a flight of stairs barking at a cat. It barked and growled, attempting to show dominance. Once the cat ran up the stairs to confront the small dog, the Pug ran away, jumping on the couch in an attempt to get away from the cat. Say-ers are just like the Pug. They try to express dominance with words, but when it's time to take responsibility for their words, they run away like cowards, forsaking their responsibilities. Do-ers don't run from anything. Do-ers stand up to any challenge brought to them.

Say-ers are dead, do-ers are not. It's just like the passage of scripture found in James chapter 2 where it references faith being dead without works. Just as works are the proof of a faith that is alive, actions are the proof that a man's word is alive. Say-ers who do not act on their word are dead, figuratively. Say-ers are dead in the sense that, after a long period of not acting on their word, their words will no longer matter. If a man's word no longer matters then it becomes vapor that is whisked away as dead leaves into the wind.

All a man has at the end of his life is the legacy he leaves behind. If you are not a man of your word, a legacy of mistrust and deceit will be left in the minds of those who knew you.

- Chapter Summary

Acting on your word isn't hard to do. All you have to do is monitor what you say and make sure you can follow through before saying it. It really isn't rocket science; it's merely wisdom. A man earns respect and trust if he practices this. Your integrity shapes others opinions of you. People may not like you as a person, but they should respect you as a man based on your ability to keep your word.

Chapter 7 - Appreciating the WoMan

- Full Disclosure

I am going to begin this chapter with a little transparency. I will let you in on my relationship with my mother, my love life and my divorce. For you to fully understand my view on appreciating a woman, you have to know my experiences.

You may be asking yourself, how can I tell you about appreciating a woman as a divorced man? Here is my response to that. As a man, I have learned from every mistake and every failure. I have grown from the boy I was when I first got married to the man I am today. I wasn't a perfect husband but I was a good husband and I loved my wife very much.

Understand that she is the mother of my three amazing sons and this will not be the "bashing the ex" portion of my book. She is deserving of honor for the mere fact that she gave birth to my sons. Thus, her reasons for leaving me will not be disclosed in this book. I will, however, share with you my shortcoming which – if it had been fixed - may have caused my wife not to leave me. As a man, I take full responsibility for my failed marriage.

I still firmly believe in marriage, and hopefully, one day I will find the right woman, according to Proverbs 31, and will be married again. I am older and wiser and I do not plan on making the same mistakes I made with the mother of my children. Until then, my focus is my relationship with God and my relationship with my children.

My mother is an amazing woman. My grandmother is even more amazing. I had the privilege to be raised by them both. My grandmother dedicated her life to me, my twin sister Alicia, my brother Anton, and my two cousins Niasha and Jacob. At the time I am writing this book, she is 87 years old and she still is very involved in our lives.

Just last week, my grandmother did the cutest thing. I told her I was going back to school and she asked me if I had a computer. I told her I had a laptop; it was old, but it would do the job. She then responded, "No, get a new one; I will give you money for a new laptop. Come to my house and I will give you $100, so you can get a new laptop." I joyfully said thank you, and thought to myself, there is no laptop that costs $100. My mother caught wind of my grandmother's generosity and she pitched in the rest of the money for the laptop.

My mother and grandmother are two of the main reasons I have such tremendous respect for women. Let me set the record straight. I am not a "momma's boy," but I do love the matriarchs in my family very much. Communicating with my mother was, and still can be, a challenge. The challenge of communicating with my mother caused me to internalize my feelings instead of voicing it, not just with my mother but with other people, as well. I overcame that, and learned that sharing how I feel is important, as long as it is done in a respectful manner. Sometimes we still butt heads, but she will always win. She is my mother, after all. She is learning that even though I will always be her son, I am no longer her "child." I am a man. I have seen my mother overcome some of the hardest situations, especially as it pertains to my relationships.

Growing up, I watched my mother and her interactions with men. I can honestly say that my mother was a noble woman. I learned how to treat women by watching the mistakes men made with my mother. My mother didn't have many relationships when I was growing up. As I recall, there were only a couple. I vowed not to put any woman through the same pain my mother went through.

Having a twin sister helped shape the level of respect I have for women, too. We are siblings, so growing up we got into our spats, some minor, some major, but all in love. Those spats helped me understand the nature of women when they argue. Women just want to be understood. We will probe deeper later in this chapter.

Heed the advice given in this chapter. Women are not going anywhere, thank God, and this chapter will help you learn how to deal with women, how to appreciate them.

Everything I learned about how to treat women was taught by my experiences with my Grandmother, Mother, Sister and my ex-Wife. The lessons in this chapter are truly lessons I apply in my own life as I deal with all women.

At my job now I am the only male among a staff of 30. Women seem to dominate the field of early childhood education. I am able to successfully work in an environment of all women because I have appreciation for women. Yes, I find women attractive, but I have learned not to let the physical attraction dictate how I treat a woman, whether they are coworkers, friends or strangers. This is something that will also benefit you as you interact with women.

- How a man ought to view women

Men are visual creatures. We are naturally drawn to what is attractive. If it can catch our eye, we want it. We react by vision more than we react by any other of the four senses. It doesn't even have to be a woman we see. Things that catch our eyes can be cars, electronics, sports, and money, to name a few. Men are moved by what they see.

My weakness is electronics. I always want the latest gadget I see. It doesn't matter what it is. If it looks bigger, brighter, faster, then I want it. I can go into an electronics store and spend hours in there looking at all the gadgets I wish I could have.

Marketing companies recognize that men are visual creatures, which is why a couple of weeks before Super Bowl there are dozens of TV and newspaper ads promoting the next best television set. They hope to sucker us into buying one for the occasion. Also, take a look at the types of commercials that air during shows targeted at men. Many of them are beer ads with half-naked women in them. What in the world does a half naked woman have to do with selling beer? Absolutely nothing. They are hoping to catch your eye just long enough for you to glimpse their product.

I believe that women are the most beautiful of God's creation. However, their beauty isn't to be lusted after. Despite what masculine society has brainwashed you into believing, women are not to be viewed as mere sexual objects. Free your mind of the subliminal messages carried in music videos, racy teen movies, magazine ads and primetime television. Do not allow yourself to fall into the thinking that women were put on this planet for your viewing pleasure only.

Realistically, a beautiful woman should catch your eye. Still, you need to learn to appreciate her beauty while not lusting after her. A pastor friend of mine says that whenever he sees a beautiful woman, he quickly acknowledges her beauty to himself and keeps it moving. It is a difficult feat, but you can do it. Seeing a woman with the figure of an acoustic guitar and staring at her while she is walking away is lust. Glaring at a woman's breasts as she is trying to talk to you isn't flattering to her; its offensive. Men ought to have control of their eyes.

Jesus said in Matthew 5:28, *"But I say to you that everyone who looks at a woman with **lust**ful intent has already committed adultery with her in his **heart.**"* Lust is a sin. This is the only sin that doesn't have to be committed physically for it to be considered a sin. Men must have a pure mind when it comes to women. Society today makes it acceptable for women to be lusted after. Even women have been fooled into thinking it is okay for men to gawk at them.

If a woman is not your wife, she ought to be viewed as your sister. We have to look at them with a sense of purity and not with a sense of personal pleasure. If a woman is your wife, you may look upon her in a sexual manner because you are in the bonds of marriage. I will get into that when I share the truth about sex.

While many would tell you it's impossible, you really do have the strength to not lust after a woman. All you have to do is tap into that reservoir of strength. In Chapter 5, I shared with you about the strength of a man's will. You must will your mind and your heart not to look at a woman in a lustful manner. Stay off pornographic websites, stay away from strip clubs and do not look at nude woman in magazines. All of that will affect you in your future relationships. There is nothing worse than being with your wife and having images of naked women flashing before your eyes. These lifestyle choices will set you up for maintaining healthy relationships with women.

- Having a healthy relationship

There is really only one thing that can guarantee a healthy relationship with a woman and that is establishing healthy boundaries. Setting up parameters that are not to be crossed will help maintain a wholesome relationship with a woman, both in a platonic and romantic context.

Boundaries keep people safe. If you are safe, then you are healthy. Everything in life has boundaries. There are consequences if those boundaries are broken. In sports, at school, at work, on the road, or even walking the streets, adhering to established boundaries will save you from needless consequences. Relationships are no different.

As a man, you must set boundaries for yourself. Set limits for yourself in the relationships you keep. If you are friends with a woman, and not seeking anything more than friendship, make sure you do not cross the boundaries you have set. Women easily mistake the kind deeds of a male friend for him being interested in her. Your friend will know your intentions up front, which will leave little to no room for misconceptions.

In romantic relationships, boundaries are especially important. They must first be set individually then agreed upon collectively in order to guarantee a healthy relationship. Boundaries will also help with understanding the intentions and expectations each has for the relationship. This will save you from disappointment. Wise men have this down cold. Strong men stick to the boundaries they have established.

Careless men cross these boundaries. Weak men run from the responsibilities.

Today, we get sucked into the label of "boyfriend." I do not believe in placing labels on relationships unless a couple is betrothed (engaged) or married. Whenever you label something, the pressure to fulfill the description creeps in. This is not to say that you shouldn't define your relationship. If you choose to court a young lady, you are doing so because it is leading to marriage. But, even in that, she isn't yet yours.

You can let her know that you are exclusively seeing her in hopes that marriage is the outcome. However, when you call a young lady your girlfriend, it carries a possessive connotation, as if to say she belongs to you. In that, the pressure for each of you to fulfill the role of a boyfriend and a girlfriend ensues, thus causing you to cross boundaries.

The Bible says that a man should leave his father and mother and hold fast to his wife, and the two shall become one flesh. I heard Pastor Mark Driscoll of Mars Hill Church explain courting in such a practical way. A young man ought to court a young lady by courting her family, as well.

Allowing her family to play a huge role in your courtship will also ensure that boundaries aren't crossed. Driscoll also advises that a young man should spend quality time alone with a young lady's parents. This will allow them to see who you are, and for them to determine whether or not you are right for their little girl. Spending time with them will also impress them.

Today, we are taught that dating is conducted between the boy and girl only. But, if there is to be any successful future, you must also get to know her family and she has to get to know yours. This may be an old-fashioned way of establishing a relationship, but it is a safe way of doing so. This helps build a healthy family and solidifies a strong support system. I will be an example of this. Should I choose to be in a relationship again, I will court my lady's family and build strong relationships with them. I will also reserve all labels for engagement.

- How to treat a woman

It is said that chivalry is dead because women killed it. If this statement is true, then it's only true because the women don't hold us to the standard of chivalry as they did in the past. Chivalry is characterized by the actions of a considerate gentleman. It is the art of making a woman feel like a lady. It has nothing to do with sex, as many men in society might lead you to believe.

When a man is chivalrous, he is marked by gracious courtesy and high-minded consideration of the fairer sex. This doesn't make him soft. It makes him a true man. The examples of adult males found in media today are not to be looked up to.

Chivalry was the characteristic that old English Knights needed to possess. For them to be Knights, they first had to prove that they were men of valor and honor. They needed to be respectful, strong and considerate, especially of women. This applied to all women - not just a spouse - and especially elderly women. Women today are in need of young knights. The independence of the contemporary woman, notwithstanding, the chivalrous knight should still live on. Here are a few things you can do to become that modern day Knight.

- o Open the doors for women. All doors. Cars included. I believe that if a lady is in the presence of a man, she should never have to open the door for herself.

- o Pull out the chair for a lady. If you see a lady going to sit down, simply offer to pull the chair out for her. When she attempts to get up out of a seat, extend your hand to assist. The same goes for women who are walking up and down stairs with no railings.

- o If you are at dinner with women, when a lady rises to excuse herself, you rise also. Ask her if she wants anything should the waiter come back around while she is away from the table.

- o Walk her to the door. Always walk a lady to her door step. This allows the woman to feel secure. Do not have any expectations of receiving a kiss if you are on a date. The 90-10 rule is reserved for movies like *Hitch*, not real life.

o Let the woman enter first. Always allow a woman to go before you. Make sure you keep your eyes up. This isn't an opportunity for you to check out the woman's backside.

o Walk with the woman and not in front of them. When you walk with a woman, it makes her feel respected rather than if you walk in front of her.

o Never put your hand on a woman to hurt her. I do not feel there is ever an excuse to strike a woman. When I was in the seventh grade, I was picked on by a girl in my class. Since the beginning of the school year, she hit and teased me continuously. In the spring, I guess I had had enough. I hit her in her face. This was the first and last time I struck a lady. I felt so disgusted with myself and realized then that, as a young man, there was a wiser way to handle that situation. Putting your hands on a woman to hurt her is never the answer.

o When you dance, dance modestly. Young men, read these next lines carefully. Learn the difference between dancing and dry humping on the dance floor. "Daggering" is not a form of dancing. Ladies should be treated with respect even on a dance floor. Simulating sex with a young lady while music is playing isn't dancing. It's being a pervert.

There are so many ways to learn how to treat a woman. I will be posting videos on this topic, as well. Make sure to visit www.therolecall.org for helpful hints on how to treat a woman.

- The basic needs of a woman

Commitment

A woman needs to know that a man is committed to her. Commitment goes way beyond being there. It involves being fully faithful. When times get hard, and they will, you as a man should not bail out and leave. Never allow another woman to take the spot that you told her she held.

Security

A woman needs to feel safe. You do not have to be a mixed martial artist to provide security for a woman; just be aware of the dangers that are around. Do not put a woman in a position where she feels uneasy or unsafe. Protect her - even if it's from you. Value her safety as if it were yours. If she is to be your wife, you must be willing to give your life for her.

Support

A woman needs to know that she is supported and provided for. This does not make her a gold digger. Provision should be a priority for a man. Also, help her as much as you can. A woman's role is not to pick up after you. This, I learned the hard way. Even though I was the sole provider in my home, my ex-wife picked up after me and not because I expected her to, but because I simply was too lazy to do it myself. She needs to know that she is more than an errand runner for you.

Conversation

A woman needs to have meaningful conversation with a man. Women like to talk. This means you must develop an affinity for listening. Not only that, you must also be willing to share your thoughts with her. Make sure you choose a woman whose voice you like to listen to. Open conversation fosters freedom in a friendship or romantic relationship.

Honesty

A woman needs to know that she is being told the truth. She needs a man that is trustworthy. It is always best to be up front and honest. This saves you from the stress of covering one lie after the other. Even if she is upset with you about the truth, she will respect you for telling it. Do not be what women believe a typical man to be. Tell the truth.

Affirmation

A woman needs words of affirmation. Take notice of her appearance. If she changes her hair color, acknowledge it, and tell her what you think of it. If she is wearing a new outfit or even if you think she looked nice in an old one, let her know. Paying non-sexual compliments to a woman is a huge part of making a woman feel better about herself.

When you are in a position to meet at least these 6 minimal needs of a woman, then I will tell you that you are on the right path to appreciating a woman.

- Chapter Summary

Women are not to be trampled on by men. Learn to respect and appreciate the female gender. You, as a man, will be so much happier if you do. Many of the things shared in this chapter are not that of popular opinion, but if you heed these words you will have peace and satisfaction in a relationship. I am far from being old-fashioned. I just know that a woman is more than just a piece of meat to lust after. Treat women with the utmost respect and that respect will be returned to you.

Chapter 8 - Sex was Invented by God

- The Origin of sex

Now, we get to the juicy stuff. I will be absolutely real and raw in this chapter. If you are a parent and do not want your son to know about this yet, then make sure he skips this chapter. However, this is something he needs to know. I would like my sons to know about this before the twisted views of modern society get to them. Sex is a topic that needs to be discussed in the home first; if you are not ready to do so, then I would be honored to broach the topic for you.

We cannot talk about sex before we discuss its original design. God made sex to be enjoyable. Sex is an experience between a man and a woman to connect with one another. When God made Eve from Adam's side, He gave Adam a charge to leave his home and become one flesh with Eve. God's reference to becoming one flesh meant for them to mate, or have sex. God blessed their union, first because He created Eve for Adam, and second because he gave them permission to have sex because they were married. You can read more about it in Genesis chapter 2.

God invented it. So, sex is not a bad thing. In fact, after He created man and woman, it was God who told them they could have sex. Sex is a good thing between a husband and his wife and that comes from the Creator Himself. So, if God says sex is good, then it is. This doesn't mean that we can step outside his guidelines for sex. Know this: God told Adam and Eve that they could have sex after they were married by God. God reserves the beauty of sex for a married couple.

In addition to vaginal penetration, sex includes oral sex, sex with objects, and even physically stimulating the genitalia of a woman or letting her stimulate yours. All of the above are acts of sex. Do not be fooled into thinking that they aren't. Still, all are blessed within the confines of marriage because the Bible says that the marriage bed is undefiled, as stated in Hebrews Chapter 13 verse 4.

On the topic of masturbation, the Bible doesn't clearly state that it is a sin. I cannot say, in good conscience, that you are sinning if you masturbate. Many use Genesis 38:9-10 (*But Onan knew that the offspring would not be his. So whenever he went in to his brother's wife he would waste the semen on the ground, so as not to give offspring to his brother. And what he did was wicked in the sight of the LORD, and he put him to death also.*) However, in its context he wasn't masturbating. He was actually having sex with her and ejaculated outside of her. What was wicked in God's sight was the deception of Onan's motives.

However, when men masturbate, the motive, the root desire is lust. Men masturbate because they are having inappropriate feelings and feel that they need a release. Even though the Bible never says that masturbation is a sin, it does clearly state that lust is a sin. Matthew 5:28 says, *"But I say to you that everyone who looks at a woman with **lustful** intent has already committed adultery with her in his heart."*

Lust is the feeling of a deep longing for something. The scripture in Matthew 5:28 is referring to looking at a woman and having feelings of sexual intent. This is the reason Jesus equates it to adultery.

Pornography is a multi-billion dollar industry because of man's lust for the female body. In this same context, men use masturbation to satisfy their lustful desires for women. There are other negative effects concerning masturbation that you can read more about by going to www.therolecall.org.

- The Beauty of Sex

For you to appreciate the true beauty of sex, you must first understand what is happening while sex is taking place. You may have thought that sex is all about you releasing and enjoying the sensation of ejaculating. Wrong. You may have even thought about the many positions you can explore while having sex. Wrong. Sex is about connecting with your wife.

This connection is referred to as a man and his wife becoming one flesh. There is much depth in that statement. It's not just an orgasm, but the joining of two bodies. If I were to explain this to a woman, they usually get it right away; it may take a little more of an explanation for you to understand.

When sex happens, this is the only time that people can actually share the same space. Through intercourse, a man and woman actually become one flesh because they literally share space with one another. This is probably the most beautiful thing about sex. This is the reason why God designed it for a husband and his wife alone.

Today's view of sex is very ugly. Sexual beauty isn't taught, nor is it even valued. The contemporary view of sex is perverted and has strayed far away from its beautiful origin. This has caused men to have a warped image of what sex is all about. Media has played a huge part in this, even to the point where they say pornography is normal and can be a healthy part of a man's sexuality. The only reason it has become the norm is because ugly sex is the norm.

Porn hurts marriages. You do not need the images of other women in your head as you are having intimate moments with your wife. Even if you do not watch porn, but you have in the past, those images are implanted in your mind and will become a memory. That is not natural. Porn isn't a means to educate you about sex either. When the time comes and you get married, things will flow and it will be beautiful. Even if you are not a virgin, it isn't too late to take a stand for abstinence and vow not to have sex until it is with your wife. Make your next sexual experience one that will be absolutely beautiful.

God's purpose for sex was to allow a man and his wife to enjoy one another while they connect. In the marriage bed, sex is a beautiful thing. Becoming one flesh is a serious thing and should not be taken lightly. Unfortunately, society today doesn't teach the beauty of sex, just how to avoid the consequences of sex.

Women view sex more deeply. Consider the physical anatomy of men and women. The main reproductive organ for a man is the penis which extends outside the body while the woman's is located inside her. During sex, a man is literally inside the woman. She feels a man on her inside while men feel a woman on his outside. Sex for a woman means allowing a man to enter inside her.

For this reason we must respect the woman's view of how beautiful sex is. Taking advantage of a woman sexually can result in extreme damage to a woman, both emotionally and physically. It is also for this reason I firmly believe sex is reserved for a husband and his wife. A husband's duty is to protect his wife, which means you must protect your wife sexually as well as physically and emotionally.

- The Consequences of sex

People, by nature, are sexual creatures. We all have urges and no one is exempt from that. These urges don't make us human. We are human and therefore we have them. Our urges don't dictate who we are; they only determine what we want. Wanting companionship and a meaningful sexual relationship isn't a bad thing.

Men weren't created like animals with only instinctive behavioral patterns. Animals do not possess the conscience to choose to act or not to act. They can be trained, but it isn't by choice. Men have the choice to act on urges. When a female mammal is in heat, the male mammals in the species will seek her out to mate with her for the purpose of reproducing. Humans are not that way. Men usually mate for the enjoyment of it, but it all boils down to a choice.

Moreover, young men have to realize the consequences of their actions, especially when they choose to have sex. Sex has both positive and negative consequences. The standard today is to ignore the positive consequences and to avoid the negative consequences. The positive consequences – and they are many - come through sex in the marriage bed, while the negative ones come through sex outside of marriage. Today, men are taught how to avoid the negative consequences rather than embracing the positive consequences.

Young man, if you are having sex with a girl and she gets pregnant, you shouldn't be surprised. The natural, God-given consequence of having sex is enjoyment and then, TADA, a baby. God also charged Adam and Eve to be fruitful and multiply. Sex produces children. Period. Today's western view of sex is rooted mainly in enjoyment and that's all. However, a baby is the ultimate fruition of two people becoming one flesh. Two individuals literally come together to make "one flesh."

Having a baby is supposed to be an occasion of joy. Bringing a life into the world is an amazing gift for a man and his wife to share. It's a positive consequence for those who desire family. To the young man seeking to just "hit it," he considers pregnancy to be a negative consequence. So, the world introduced condoms and other methods of birth control to combat the natural reaction to sex.

Too many young men are disappointed when they have sex and they find out their sex partner is pregnant. That's not supposed to be the case at all. In a marriage, a husband would get excited when his wife tells him they are having a baby. It means that their family is expanding and he will be leaving a legacy.

Sex is the glue that bonds a married couple, but it is the bomb that completely destroys a budding relationship. Sex can create life and it can destroy it. "You are having a baby and now your life is ruined" is quoted to many new, unmarried parents. "You are having a baby, what a blessing" is quoted to married parents, excited about the new edition to their family.

Sex is fun but wasn't meant for recreation alone. Men tend to think of sex as another means of recreation. Our young men are truly misguided when it comes to this. They are told to strap on a condom and keep it moving.

Condoms are nothing but a way to escape the natural consequences of having sex. Young men are celebrated for having multiple sex partners by their older male role models. NOT IN MY HOUSE. My sons will be celebrated for abstaining and saving themselves for their wives.

The truth of the matter is that an orgasm feels good. An orgasm occurs at the peak of a man or woman's sexual encounter. It's an intense explosive discharge that makes a man ejaculate. Regardless of the intense feeling a man gets while having sex, the amazing feeling isn't an excuse to have sex recreationally. Recreational sex is having sex just for the fun of it. Usually this entails one night stands and friends with benefits. Both of these cheapen the meaning for why sex was created in the first place, and that is for a connection between a man and his wife.

Finally, we cannot discuss consequences without talking about the many diseases transmitted through sex. More than 20 STD's (sexually transmitted diseases) can be contracted through irresponsible sexual relations. This includes intercourse, oral sex, and manual stimulation. The Illinois Department of Public Health reports that each year over 12 million new cases of STD's are diagnosed in the United States. They also report that on average 2 teens are infected with HIV every hour in the United States alone.

These are serious and scary statistics. The reason we have such horrendous consequences to sex is because the intended purpose for sex has been perverted. There are ugly consequences for ugly sex and beautiful consequences for beautiful sex. We need to learn to appreciate sex in all its beauty. Knowing your value as a man will help you understand its beauty.

- Know your value as a man

Do not let sex control you. It takes more strength to abstain until marriage than it does to give in to your youthful lusts. The Bible says to flee youthful lusts in 2 Timothy 2:22. Run away like your life and the life of another depends on it because, quite frankly, they do. Take on the mindset that what you have to offer is good and not just any "chick" can have access to it. You've got to give the goods to the one woman who has proven herself worthy.

You have to consider the sex you are giving to a woman as something special. Only one woman should be worthy of getting the goods that you offer. You should consider yourself priceless. The more accessible something is, the less it's worth. If you have sex with as many girls as you can, then your sex is worthless. The beauty of the moments you share with your wife become cheapened. Not to mention, if you contract a disease, then your sex isn't worth having at all. No one wants it then.

Wouldn't you want to give your wife something more valuable than any ring you can offer her? Wouldn't you like to give her something that no other woman has ever received? That one special gift that you can give her is your virginity -- your mind and body in a state that is uncompromised.

I wish I had someone to teach me this before I gave my heart and life to God at age 17. It would have saved me from a lot of emotional hurt and heartbreak. Treat sex with respect. If you want to have good sex, make sure to follow God's design for sex. And when you do get married, make sure every time you are intimate with your wife, have the time of your life.

- Chapter Summary

Sex is God given; however, He has a divine purpose for it. It was designed to be a fun way for a husband and his wife to connect with one another. Sex is not a bad word. You do not have to follow the footsteps that society has placed down for you.

Desire to have the best sex you can have. It's the type of sex that God designed you to have. You aren't a punk or a sissy if you choose to wait. In fact, you are more of a man for waiting to have sex with your wife. Waiting shows a great deal of strength and self control. You got this. You control sex. Do not let sex control you.

Chapter 9 – They're Your Children Not Your Inconvenience

- The Importance Of A Father

The term "father" was never meant to be a term used loosely for men who merely produce the sperm cells to make a baby. Father is now considered a fluid term that no longer carries with it the meaning of male caregiver. Talk shows known for catch phrases like "You Are" or "You Are Not The Father" are further proof that "father" is no longer a word that is taken seriously in our society.

In a recent conversation I had with an acquaintance, we mulled over the definition of the word father. We got into semantics, whether it meant a term for a man who has the legal rights to his child by way of biology or by way of adoption. We also argued about whether every man who produced a biological child should be deemed a father. My view was no. Her view was yes. She based her view on biology while I based mine on behavior.

She argued that every child has a father. I argued that every child has a man who produced the sperm that made them. Then, she posited, "what about the mother?" To which I responded, "So **what** if she was in labor for 20 hours, surrogates do it all the time! If she doesn't care for her children, she is not a mother, just like if a man doesn't care for his children he is not a father."

Parenting isn't automatic. To prove said point, we need not look any further than all of the world's fatherless children, me included. This may be my personal view, but it's a view I developed out of my own experience. If you are labeled as something, then it's because you act on that label. A drug addict takes drugs habitually. A teacher instructs students in a classroom. A filmmaker creates movies. Whenever a person is classified in a particular role, it's because they have done something tangible. The same goes for the role of a parent.

Something as important as fatherhood shouldn't be attributed to a man merely because he had sex with a woman and impregnated her. Fatherhood should hold much more weight than that.

Fathers are important, not just in the lives of their children, but in society on a whole. The moral decline of today's generation is due in part to the lack of fathers playing an active role. And when I say "in part," I mean a big part. Here are some staggering statistics to prove this claim. (Taken from The National Fatherhood Initiative www.fatherhood.org)

Data on the Consequences of Father Absence

According to the <u>U.S. Census Bureau</u>, 24 million children in America -- one out of three -- live in biological father-absent homes.

Consequently, there is a "father factor" in nearly all of the social issues facing America today.

The following is data on the effects of father absence on: poverty, maternal and child health, incarceration, crime, teen pregnancy, child abuse, drug and alcohol abuse, education, and childhood obesity.

Father Factor in Poverty

- Children in father-absent homes are five times more likely to be poor. In 2002, 7.8 percent of children in married-couple families were living in poverty, compared to 38.4 percent of children in female-householder families.

  Source: U.S. Census Bureau, Children's Living Arrangements and Characteristics: March 2002, P200-547, Table C8. Washington D.C.: GPO, 2003.

- During the year before their babies were born, 43% of unmarried mothers received welfare or food stamps, 21% received some type of housing subsidy, and 9% received another type of government transfer (unemployment insurance etc.). For women who have another child, the proportion who receive welfare or food stamps rises to 54%.

Source: McLanahan, Sara. The Fragile Families and Child Well-being Study: Baseline National Report. Princeton, NJ: Center for Research on Child Well-being, 2003: 13.

- A child with a nonresident father is 54 percent more likely to be poorer than his or her father.

Source: Sorenson, Elaine and Chava Zibman. "Getting to Know Poor Fathers Who Do Not Pay Child Support." Social Service Review 75 (September 2001): 420-434.

- When compared by family structure, 45.9% of poor single-parent families reported material hardship compared to 38.6% of poor two parent families. For unpoor families who did not experience material hardship, 23.3% were single-parent families compared to 41.2% of two-parent families.

Source: Beverly, Sondra G., "Material hardship in the United States: Evidence from the Survey of Income and Program Participation." Social Work Research 25 (September 2001): 143-151.3

Father Factor in Maternal and Infant Health

- Infant mortality rates are 1.8 times higher for infants of unmarried mothers than for married mothers.

Source: Matthews, T.J., Sally C. Curtin, and Marian F. MacDorman. Infant Mortality Statistics from the 1998 Period Linked Birth/Infant Death Data Set.

National Vital Statistics Reports, Vol. 48, No. 12. Hyattsville, MD: National Center for Health Statistics, 2000.

- Based on birth and death data for 217,798 children born in Georgia in 1989 and 1990, infants without a father's name on their birth certificate (17.9 percent of the total) were 2.3 times more likely to die in the first year of life compared to infants with a father's name on their birth certificate.

  Source: Gaudino, Jr., James A., Bill Jenkins, and Foger W. Rochat. "No Fathers' Names: A Risk Factor for Infant Mortality in the State of Georgia, USA." Social Science and Medicine 48 (1999): 253-265.

- Unmarried mothers are less likely to obtain prenatal care and more likely to have a low birth-weight baby. Researchers find that these negative effects persist even when they take into account factors, such as parental education, that often distinguish single-parent from two-parent families.

  Source: U.S. Department of Health and Human Services. Public Health Service. Center for Disease Control and Prevention. National Center for Health Statistics. Report to Congress on Out-of-Wedlock Childbearing. Hyattsville, MD (Sept. 1995): 12.

- Expectant fathers can play a powerful role as advocates of breastfeeding to their wives. Three-fourths of women whose partners attended a breastfeeding promotion class initiated breastfeeding.

Source: Wolfberg, Adam J., et al. "Dads as breastfeeding advocates: results from a randomized controlled trial of an educational intervention." American Journal of Obstetrics and Gynecology 191 (September 2004): 708-712.

• Fathers' knowledge about breastfeeding increases the likelihood that a child will be breastfed. Children who fathers knew more had a 1.76 higher chance of being breastfed at the end of the first month and 1.91 higher chance of receiving maternal milk at the end of the third month.

Source: Susin, Lurie R.O. "Does Parental Breastfeeding Knowledge Increase Breastfeeding Rates?" BIRTH 26 (September 1999): 149-155.

• Twenty-three percent of unmarried mothers in large U.S. cities reported cigarette use during their pregnancy. Seventy-one percent were on Medicare.

Source: McLanahan, Sara. The Fragile Families and Child Well-being Study: Baseline National Report. Table 7. Princeton, NJ: Center for Research on Child Well-being, 2003: 16.

• A study of 2,921 mothers revealed that single mothers were twice as likely as married mothers to experience a bout of depression in the prior year. Single mothers also reported higher levels of stress, fewer contacts with family and friends, less involvement with church or social groups and less overall social support.

Source: Cairney, John and Michael Boyle et al. "Stress, Social Support and Depression in Single and Married Mothers." Social Psychiatry and Psychiatric Epidemiology 38 (August 2003): 442-449.

- In a longitudinal study of more than 10,000 families, researchers found that toddlers living in stepfamilies and single-parent families were more likely to suffer a burn, have a bad fall, or be scarred from an accident compared to kids living with both of their biological parents.

Source: O'Connor, T., L. Davies, J. Dunn, J. Golding, ALSPAC Study Team. "Differential Distribution of Children's Accidents, Injuries and Illnesses across Family Type." Pediatrics 106 (November 2000): e68.

- A study of 3,400 middle schoolers indicated that not living with both biological parents quadruples the risk of having an affective disorder.

Source: Cuffe, Steven P., Robert E. McKeown, Cheryl L. Addy, and Carol Z. Garrison. "Family Psychosocial Risk Factors in a Longitudinal Epidemiological Study of Adolescents." Journal of American Academic Child Adolescent Psychiatry 44 (February 2005): 121-129.

- Children who live apart from their fathers are more likely to be diagnosed with asthma and experience an asthma-related emergency even after taking into account demographic and socioeconomic conditions. Unmarried, cohabiting parents and unmarried parents living apart are 1.76 and 2.61 times, respectively, more likely to have their child diagnosed with asthma. Marital disruption after birth is associated with a 6-fold increase in the likelihood a children will require an emergency room visit and 5-fold increase of an asthma-related emergency.

Source: Harknett, Kristin. Children's Elevated Risk of Asthma in Unmarried Families: Underlying Structural and Behavioral Mechanisms. Working Paper #2005-01-FF. Princeton, NJ: Center for Research on Child Well-being, 2005: 19-27.

Father Factor in Incarceration

- Even after controlling for income, youths in father-absent households still had significantly higher odds of incarceration than those in mother-father families. Youths who never had a father in the household experienced the highest odds.

Source: Harper, Cynthia C. and Sara S. McLanahan. "Father Absence and Youth Incarceration." Journal of Research on Adolescence 14 (September 2004): 369-397.

- A 2002 Department of Justice survey of 7,000 inmates revealed that 39% of jail inmates lived in mother-only households. Approximately forty-six percent of jail inmates in 2002 had a previously incarcerated family member. One-fifth experienced a father in prison or jail.

Source: James, Doris J. Profile of Jail Inmates, 2002. (NCJ 201932). Bureau of Justice Statistics Special Report, Department of Justice, Office of Justice Programs, July 2004.

Father Factor in Crime

- A study of 109 juvenile offenders indicated that family structure significantly predicts delinquency.

  Source: Bush, Connee, Ronald L. Mullis, and Ann K. Mullis. "Differences in Empathy Between Offender and Nonoffender Youth." Journal of Youth and Adolescence 29 (August 2000): 467-478.

- Adolescents, particularly boys, in single-parent families were at higher risk of status, property and person delinquencies. Moreover, students attending schools with a high proportion of children of single parents are also at risk.

  Source: Anderson, Amy L. "Individual and contextual influences on delinquency: the role of the single-parent family." Journal of Criminal Justice 30 (November 2002): 575-587.

- A study of 13,986 women in prison showed that more than half grew up without their father. Forty-two percent grew up in a single-mother household and sixteen percent lived with neither parent. (Fathers and Daughters)

  Source: Snell, Tracy L and Danielle C. Morton. Women in Prison: Survey of Prison Inmates, 1991. Bureau of

Justice Statistics Special Report. Washington, DC: US Department of Justice, 1994: 4.

- Even after controlling for community context, there is significantly more drug use among children who do not live with their mother and father.

  Source: Hoffmann, John P. "The Community Context of Family Structure and Adolescent Drug Use." Journal of Marriage and Family 64 (May 2002): 314-330.

- Youths are more at risk of first substance use without a highly involved father. Each unit increase in father involvement is associated with 1% reduction in substance use. Living in an intact family also decreases the risk of first substance use.

  Source: Bronte-Tinkew, Jacinta, Kristin A. Moore, Randolph C. Capps, and Jonathan Zaff. "The influence of father involvement on youth risk behaviors among adolescents: A comparison of native-born and immigrant families." Article in Press. Social Science Research December 2004.

- Of the 228 students studied, those from single-parent families reported higher rates of drinking and smoking as well as higher scores on delinquency and aggression tests when compared to boys from two-parent households.

  Source: Griffin, Kenneth W., Gilbert J. Botvin, Lawrence M. Scheier, Tracy Diaz and Nicole L. Miller.

"Parenting Practices as Predictors of Substance Use, Delinquency, and Aggression Among Urban Minority Youth: Moderating Effects of Family Structure and Gender." Psychology of Addictive Behaviors 14 (June 2000): 174-184.

- In a study of INTERPOL crime statistics of 39 countries, it was found that single parenthood ratios were strongly correlated with violent crimes. This was not true 18 years ago.

Source: Barber, Nigel. "Single Parenthood As a Predictor of Cross-National Variation in Violent Crime." Cross-Cultural Research 38 (November 2004): 343-358.

Father Factor in Teen Pregnancy

- Being raised by a single mother raises the risk of teen pregnancy, marrying with less than a high school degree, and forming a marriage where both partners have less than a high school degree.

Source: Teachman, Jay D. "The Childhood Living Arrangements of Children and the Characteristics of Their Marriages." Journal of Family Issues 25 (January 2004): 86-111.

- Separation or frequent changes increase a woman's risk of early menarche, sexual activity and pregnancy. Women whose parents separated between birth and six years old experienced twice the risk of early menstruation, more than four times the risk of early sexual intercourse, and two and a half times higher risk of early pregnancy when compared to women in intact families. The longer a woman lived with both parents, the lower her risk of early reproductive development. Women who experienced three or more changes in her family environment exhibited similar risks but were five times more likely to have an early pregnancy.

Source: Quinlan, Robert J. "Father absence, parental care, and female reproductive development." Evolution and Human Behavior 24 (November 2003): 376-390.

- Researchers using a pool from both the U.S. and New Zealand found strong evidence that father absence has an effect on early sexual activity and teenage pregnancy. Teens without fathers were twice as likely to be involved in early sexual activity and seven times more likely to get pregnant as an adolescent.

Source: Ellis, Bruce J., John E. Bates, Kenneth A. Dodge, David M. Ferguson, L. John Horwood, Gregory S. Pettit, and Lianne Woodward. "Does Father Absence Place Daughters at Special Risk for Early Sexual Activity and Teenage Pregnancy." Child Development 74 (May/June 2003): 801-821.

Father Factor in Child Abuse

- Compared to living with both parents, living in a single-parent home doubles the risk that a child will suffer physical, emotional, or educational neglect.

Source: America's Children: Key National Indicators of Well-Being. Table SPECIAL1. Washington, D.C.: Federal Interagency Forum on Child and Family Statistics, 1997.

- The overall rate of child abuse and neglect in single-parent households is 27.3 children per 1,000, whereas the rate of overall maltreatment in two-parent households is 15.5 per 1,000.

Source: America's Children: Key National Indicators of Well-Being. Table SPECIAL1. Washington, D.C.: Federal Interagency Forum on Child and Family Statistics, 1997.

- An analysis of child abuse cases in a nationally representative sample of 42 counties found that children from single-parent families are more likely to be victims of physical and sexual abuse than children who live with both biological parents. Compared to their peers living with both parents, children in single parent homes had:
  - a 77% greater risk of being physically abused
  - an 87% greater risk of being harmed by physical neglect
  - a 165% greater risk of experiencing notable physical neglect
  - a 74% greater risk of suffering from emotional neglect
  - an 80% greater risk of suffering serious injury as a result of abuse
  - overall, a 120% greater risk of being endangered by some type of child abuse.

Source: Sedlak, Andrea J. and Diane D. Broadhurst. The Third National Incidence Study of Child Abuse and Neglect: Final Report. U.S. Department of Health and Human Services. National Center on Child Abuse and Neglect. Washington, D.C., September 1996.

Father Factor in Drug and Alcohol Abuse

- Researchers at Columbia University found that children living in two-parent household with a poor relationship with their father are 68% more likely to smoke, drink, or use drugs compared to all teens in two-parent households. Teens in single mother households are at a 30% higher risk than those in two-parent households.

  Source: "Survey Links Teen Drug Use, Relationship With Father." Alcoholism & Drug Abuse Weekly 6 September 1999: 5.

- Even after controlling for community context, there is significantly more drug use among children who do not live with their mother and father.

  Source: Hoffmann, John P. "The Community Context of Family Structure and Adolescent Drug Use." Journal of Marriage and Family 64 (May 2002): 314-330.

- In a study of 6,500 children from the ADDHEALTH database, father closeness was negatively correlated with the number of a child's friends who smoke, drink, and smoke marijuana.

Closeness was also correlated with a child's use of alcohol, cigarettes, and hard drugs and was connected to family structure. Intact families ranked higher on father closeness than single-parent families.

Source: National Fatherhood Initiative. "Family Structure, Father Closeness, & Drug Abuse." Gaithersburg, MD: National Fatherhood Initiative, 2004: 20-22.

- Of the 228 students studied, those from single-parent families reported higher rates of drinking and smoking as well as higher scores on delinquency and aggression tests when compared to boys from two-parent households.

Source: Griffin, Kenneth W., Gilbert J. Botvin, Lawrence M. Scheier, Tracy Diaz and Nicole L. Miller. "Parenting Practices as Predictors of Substance Use, Delinquency, and Aggression Among Urban Minority Youth: Moderating Effects of Family Structure and Gender." Psychology of Addictive Behaviors 14 (June 2000): 174-184.

Father Factor in Childhood Obesity

- The National Longitudinal Survey of Youth found that obese children are more likely to live in father-absent homes than are non-obese children.

Source: National Longitudinal Survey of Youth

- Study that looked at family lifestyle and parent's Body Mass Index (BMI) over a nine year period found:
  - Father's Body Mass Index (BMI) predicts son's and daughter's BMI independent of offspring's alcohol intake, smoking, physical fitness, and father's education
  - Furthermore, BMI in sons and daughters consistently higher when fathers were overweight or obese
  - Physical fitness of daughters negatively related to their father's obesity
  - Obesity of fathers associated with a four-fold increase in the risk of obesity of sons and daughters at age 18

Source: Burke V, Beilin LJ, Dunbar D. "Family lifestyle and parental body mass index as predictors of body mass index in Australian children: a longitudinal study." Department of Medicine, Royal Perth Hospital, University of Western Australia, and the Western Australian Heart Research Institute; Perth, Australia.

- A fathers' body mass index (a measurement of the relative composition of fat and muscle mass in the human body) is directly related to a child's activity level. In a study of 259 toddlers, more active children were more likely to have a father with a lower BMI than less active children.

Source: Finn, Kevin, Neil Johannsen, and Bonny Specker. "Factors associated with physical activity in preschool children." The Journal of Pediatrics 140 (January 2002): 81-85.

- A study that looked at dietary intake and physical activity of parents and their daughters over a two year period found:
  - ○ Daughter's BMI predicted by father's diets and father's enjoyment of physical activity
  - ○ As father's BMI rose, so did their daughter's BMI

Source: Davison KK, Birch LL. "Child and parent characteristics as predictors of change in girls' body mass index." Department of Human Development and Family Studies, The Pennsylvania State University, University Park, Pennsylvania 16802, USA.

- Study that looked at the relationship between parent's total and percentage body fat and daughter's total body fat over a two and one-half year period found: Father's, not mother's, total and percentage body fat the best predictor of changes in daughter's total and percentage body fat.

Source: Figueroa-Colon R, Arani RB, Goran MI, Weinsier RL. "Paternal body fat is a longitudinal predictor of changes in body fat in premenarcheal girls." Department of Pediatrics, General Clinical Research Center, Medical Statistics Unit, Comprehensive Cancer Center, University of Alabama at Birmingham, USA.

- Two studies that have looked at the determinants of physical activity in obese and non-obese children found:
  - Obese children less likely to report that their father's were physically active than were the children of non-obese children. This determinant not found for mothers.
  - Father's inactivity strong predictor of children's inactivity.

Source: Trost SG, Kerr LM, Ward DS, Pate RR. "Physical activity and determinants of physical activity in obese and non-obese children. School of Human Movement Studies, The University of Queensland, Brisbane, Queensland 4072, Australia. Source: Fogelholm M, Nuutinen O, Pasanen M, Myohanen E, Saatela T. "Parent-child relationship of physical activity patterns and obesity." University of Helsinki, Lahti Research and Training Centre, Finland.

- Children who lived with single mothers were significantly more likely to become obese by a 6-year follow-up, as were black children, children with nonworking parents, children with nonprofessional parents, and children whose mothers did not complete high school.

Source: Strauss RS, Knight J. "Influence of the home environment on the development of obesity in children." Division of Pediatric Gastroenterology and Nutrition, University of Medicine and Dentistry of New Jersey, Robert Wood Johnson School of Medicine, New Brunswick, New Jersey 08903, USA.

Father Factor in Education

- Fatherless children are twice as likely to drop out of school.

  Source: U.S. Department of Health and Human Services. National Center for Health Statistics. Survey on Child Health. Washington, D.C.: GPO, 1993.

- Father involvement in schools is associated with the higher likelihood of a student getting mostly A's. This was true for fathers in biological parent families, for stepfathers, and for fathers heading single-parent families.

  Source: Nord, Christine Winquist, and Jerry West. Fathers' and Mothers' Involvement in Their Children's Schools by Family Type and Resident Status. (NCES 2001-032). Washington, D.C.: U.S. Department of Education, National Center for Education Statistics, 2001.

- Students living in father-absent homes are twice as likely to repeat a grade in school; 10 percent of children living with both parents have ever repeated a grade, compared to 20 percent of children in stepfather families and 18 percent in mother-only families.

  Source: Nord, Christine Winquist, and Jerry West. Fathers' and Mothers' Involvement in Their Children's Schools by Family Type and Resident Status. (NCES 2001-032). Washington, D.C.: U.S. Department of Education, National Center for Education Statistics, 2001.

- Students in single-parent families or stepfamilies are significantly less likely than students living in intact families to have parents involved in their schools. About half of students living in single-parent families or stepfamilies have parents who are highly involved, while 62 percent of students living with both their parents have parents who are highly involved in their schools.

  Source: Nord, Christine Winquist, and Jerry West. Fathers' and Mothers' Involvement in Their Children's Schools by Family Type and Resident Status. (NCES 2001-032). Washington, D.C.: U.S. Department of Education, National Center for Education Statistics, 2001.

- In 2001, 61 percent of 3- to 5-year olds living with two parents were read aloud to everyday by a family member, compared to 48% of children living in single- or no-parent families.

  Source: Federal Interagency Forum on Child and Family Statistics. America's Children: Key National Indicators of Well-Being, 2002. Table ED1. Washington, DC: U.S. Government Printing Office, 2003.

- Kindergarteners who live with single-parents are over-represented in those lagging in health, social and emotional, and cognitive outcomes. Thirty-three percent of children who were behind in all three areas were living with single parents while only 22% were not lagging behind.

Source: Wertheimer, Richard and Tara Croan, et al. Attending Kindergarten and Already Behind: A Statistical Portrait of Vulnerable Young Children. Child Trends Research Brief. Publication #2003-20. Washington, DC: Child Trends, 2003.

- In two-parent families, children under the age of 13 spend an average of 1.77 hours engaged in activities with their fathers and 2.35 hours doing so with their mothers on a daily basis in 1997. Children in single parent families spent on .42 hours with their fathers and 1.26 hours with their mothers on daily basis.

Source: Lippman, Laura, et al. Indicators of Child, Family, and Community Connections. Office of the Assistant Secretary for Planning and Evaluation. Washington, DC: US Department of Health and Human Services, 2004.

- A study of 1330 children from the PSID showed that fathers who are involved on a personal level with their child schooling increases the likelihood of their child's achievement. When fathers assume a positive role in their child's education, students feel a positive impact.

Source: McBride, Brent A., Sarah K. Schoppe-Sullivan, and Moon-Ho Ho. "The mediating role of fathers' school involvement on student achievement." Applied Developmental Psychology 26 (2005): 201-216.

- Half of all children with highly involved fathers in two-parent families reported getting mostly A's through 12th grade, compared to 35.2% of children of nonresident father families.

Source: National Center for Education Statistics. The Condition of Education. NCES 1999022. Washington, DC: U.S. Dept. of Education, 1999: 76.

Now that we know the stats, we need not have any qualms about taking steps to rectify this issue. It's not enough for a man just to pay child support; children need the active presence of their father in their lives. If you are a man who just pays child support, then let's call a spade a spade. You are a "sperm donor."

There isn't one perfect father but there are a lot of amazing fathers out there. What makes a father different than a sperm donor is that a father "acts." Fathers need to take the time to help with homework, teach their children how to ride a bike, play sports with them, talk about the emotional issues children face, and even lovingly enforce the boundaries established in the homes. If you are man enough to have sex with a woman, then you should be man enough to care for the natural consequences of your manly action.

In all truth, having sex doesn't make you a man. You are a man, however, if you care for what I see as a joyous consequence of the sex. I have heard men say "I didn't ask for this." OH, YES YOU DID!!! The 2-10 minutes of pleasure you agreed to when you had sex with this woman was when you asked to have a baby. Remember, a baby is **supposed** to happen after sex. It's not an accident. Sex is the first step in the reproductive process.

Man up. Do what you have to do as a father. Our society needs it, your children's mother needs it, and your children need it. No more copping out. It isn't too late for you to take the role that you are supposed to play in your children's life. Even if your "baby's momma" gives you a hard time, this is the one instance where I will tell you to fight her. Not with weapons that will hurt her physically or emotionally, but with the law.

The law protects a father's right to be active in the lives of his children. Do not let a bitter, angry woman drive you away from giving your children the essential love and support they need from a father. Even if you have to deal with her drama, it will be well worth it because your children will be better off. Stop being a punk. If you are in a situation where your children's mother is giving you a hard time, never run away. Take your place and stand in the role you were meant to play. A Father.

Google "Support for Fathers" and research the many resources available to you out there.

I want to encourage you to visit the website at www.fatherhood.org. You will find a vast amount of resources that will help fathers be more effective in the lives of their children. Even if you have never met your children, it is never too late. To the mothers reading this, please encourage the involvement of your children's father. Regardless of the differences you two may have had, the children should not bear the brunt of the repercussions.

- Accepting Responsibility At Any Cost

Real men will stand up to their responsibility. As I am writing the words on these pages, I am newly separated from the ministry I was overseeing. I was afforded additional tasks that had me in the office from 9am-5pm every day of the week, back at the church Tuesday-Friday evenings, every Sunday for 6 hours and 2 Saturdays a month. As a single father of three, I could not take on the added responsibilities because my first ministry was to my children. As a result, I had to resign from my position.

A father's first priority is to his family, not his job or ministry. Making your occupation your priority will damage the structure and well-being of your family. A father ought to be the foundation of the family. Your first responsibility, contrary to what some may have told you, is not just to provide food, clothing and a place for them to live. Additionally, not having custody of your children isn't an excuse for a father to shirk the responsibilities he has to his children.

I actually know of fathers who will never leave work if their children are sick because they believe they pay child support for their children's mother to do that. I have to be honest; some fathers literally make me sick. I get SICK to my stomach and my brain. I look at my children and would never cast off these sorts of responsibilities to their mother.

Young man, if you are grown enough to have sex with a woman, you have to be man enough to take on the mutual responsibility of raising a child with her. Accept the highest responsibility a man can have: fatherhood. If you have impregnated a woman, take on the honor of being the most important person in that child's life. The cost of your responsibility is worth the end product. That end product is a child growing up with the knowledge that he/she is worth the time, love and affection of their father.

Chapter Summary

Fatherhood isn't a light task but it is worth the challenge. The statistics speak for themselves. The presence of a father, or a positive male role model, is important in the life of a child.

Whether you are a young man about to be a father, a single mother, or even a father who has been absent in your child's life, please know that men are needed in rearing up children. A father's role and responsibility is just as important as a mother's role and responsibility in a child's life.

Chapter 10 - Leaving a Legacy

You are now in the final chapter of the book. Whether you are a young man, single mom or father looking to reconnect to his kids, I hope this book has sparked a charge in you to leave a legacy behind.

- What is a Man of Legacy

Webster's definition of legacy is "something transmitted by or received from an ancestor or predecessor or from the past." For you to understand what a man of legacy is, you first have to know what a legacy is. It is a gift that your children and children's children will relish in and enjoy when you are long gone. I am going to clarify my position in this portion of the chapter by offering you examples of men who have left legacies for their succeeding generations.

Throughout history, we hear stories of men who have changed the course of history which, in turn, changed generations behind them. Men who are legacy-minded all share a common goal and that is to change a generation. The goal I set out to achieve in writing this book is to help change the generation of men behind me and to encourage them to be men of legacy.

To be a man of legacy is to be a man whose ideals are so powerful that they live on far beyond the death of this man. Martin Luther, Martin Luther King, Jr., Abraham

Lincoln and Mahatma Gandhi. Even those whose ideals have negatively affected following generations such as Hitler were men of legacy, too. Their twisted beliefs live on in others. Research the men named in this paragraph and learn how they impacted generations behind them. Are your ideals so strong that they would live long beyond your death?

Not every man leaves behind a legacy for their successor, but every man should. A man should leave a gift for the people behind him to carry on in a man's absence. Earlier in the book, I mentioned a man who told me not to teach everything I know to someone else because it would render me replaceable. The man who told me that doesn't have a legacy mindset.

A man who is secure in himself isn't worried about being replaced. His concern is when he is gone, will the work continue? My goal as a man is to teach my sons everything that I know so that, in my absence, they can continue to live out the legacy I've left. I know that I will not live forever and my sons will have the memories of the lessons that I taught them. Do not be afraid to think bigger than yourself. This is the first step of living a legacy. You must learn to live beyond yourself.

- Living Beyond Yourself

Everyone who has picked up this book is an important individual. You have picked up this book because you seek to learn more about manhood. But, frankly, it will mean nothing if you choose not to pass it on.

To live beyond yourself means to extend yourself to other people. With this act, you acknowledge that people's lives are worth pouring into. We must all come to terms with the idea that our lives aren't only about ourselves, but they are also about those who we encounter on a daily basis.

Many people, men and women, go about their daily lives only to seek to advance themselves. This is the action of someone who has not fully understood the idea of what living is really about. Life is best lived when you are doing for others not just yourself. In South Africa, there is the tribal philosophy of Ubuntu, which means that I am who I am because of who you are. Archbishop Desmond Tutu expounded on this poignant concept native to his homeland:

> *One of the sayings in our country is Ubuntu – the essence of being human. Ubuntu speaks particularly about the fact that you can't exist as a human being in isolation. It speaks about our interconnectedness. You can't be human all by yourself, and when you have this quality – Ubuntu – you are known for your generosity. We think of ourselves far too frequently as just individuals, separated from one another, whereas you are connected and what you do affects the whole World. When you do well, it spreads out; it is for the whole of humanity.*

Ubuntu would affirm that that there is no such thing as a selfless deed because even in a deed that is supposedly selfless, you are made to feel good by doing it because you have made someone else feel good. As you do deeds for other people, you pour into them. You are not only doing a good thing. You are living beyond yourself.

This is a difficult thing for men to do sometimes because men are accustomed to doing things for themselves to better their own situations. In the corporate world, men will lie, cheat, steal, stab each other in the back and even kiss up to get a leg up on their competitor. By nature, men can be very competitive. But when you have decided to live beyond yourself, it is no longer about making yourself better. It is about making the world better. You cannot be a cutthroat person and seek to live beyond yourself.

This principle, I believe, can change the world if it is applied by all men. This is a part of leaving a legacy: to live beyond yourself and to extend yourself to others. You must never ignore the people around you. Even the Bible says that people should be the "salt of the earth." If the salt loses its flavor, then it is good for nothing but to be trampled over. Simply, if others cannot taste your success and gain from it, then you too are good for nothing.

To the young men reading this book, I beg of you: do not grow up with the notion that you've got only yourself to worry about. That is one of the reasons why you may not have your father in your life right now. Your absent father may have thought it would be better for him to leave and only worry about himself. Now, I know in some situations the mom has driven the father away. But even in that, the mom thought it would be better for her – in the end – if this man wasn't around. Both are selfish acts that may well have had a negative effect on you growing up.

It's time for a change. It's time for a shift. It's time for young men like you to begin living beyond yourself.

- Multiplying Yourself

I have three sons that bear my last name. I feel a sense of pride that there are three young men who will be carrying on my last name after I pass away. However, it's not enough that I have sons that bear my last name.

Having children to carry on a name from generation to generation shouldn't be the peak of a man's pride. I have heard stories of men walking out on their children because the mother didn't give their child their last name. I have also heard stories of men who are proud to have children bear their last name yet do nothing to help support the child. A name is just a title that will die with you, but lessons transcend time.

Everybody has something to teach another. When you share with others the lessons you have learned, you multiply yourself. There are many ways I seek to multiply myself and this book is one of them. Just as I have learned lessons that I wish to teach to my sons, you have valuable insights that need to be shared with others.

The concept of multiplying yourself is the same as simple mathematics. You can start off by sharing some of your insights to 5 people. Those 5 people can possibly share it with another 5 people then you have 25 people who you have multiplied you. If those 25 people shared the insight you gave to the initial 5 then you have multiplied yourself to 125 people. And if those 125 shared it with 5, then you have affected 625 people. 5x5x5x5=625.

Multiplying yourself is simply sharing what you know with others and giving them the opportunity to do the same. This means you have to figuratively leave the skin of your own body and become an idea, an idea that is contagious and infects others around you. Martin Luther King is known for a dream he had about the uniting of all races. His idea multiplied and he left his own skin to impact many. Real men aren't afraid to offer a little piece of themselves for another's benefit.

Multiplication of your ideals is all about being a man of legacy. The more you share the lessons you learned with others, the more they will share them with those they come across. Just make sure what you share has value.

Earlier, I shared with you about valuing your word. If you want to share words that mean nothing such as senseless gossip, hate, or discourse then all you will leave with people is the idea that you are a selfish, uncaring, hateful man. Make sure the ideas and values you wish to multiply have substance and meaning. They should be words that will positively benefit the hearer so they can positively impact someone else.

- Be A Legend

One of my favorite comic book characters is Batman. Batman is one of the most feared and respected heroes in DC comics and doesn't have super human abilities. Bruce Wayne, who is Batman without the mask, is a man seeking to make a difference. Batman earned every skill he has through hard work and determination. Even Superman, who is arguably the most powerful superhero, respects Batman and will submit to Batman's leadership.

In the 2005 movie, Batman Begins, Henri Ducard/ Ras Al Guhl tells Bruce Wayne, "If you make yourself more than just a man, if you devote yourself to an ideal and if they can't stop you, you become something else entirely - legend, Mr. Wayne."

A legend is a story handed down from generation to generation. Legends may evolve but all legends have an origin. Ideals are the same way. Lessons are taught and should be shared to each coming generation. Men cannot leave the next generation destitute of knowledge that can help them grow and find their destiny.

The Torah, the Jewish Bible, is legendary and the men and women mentioned in it are legendary. The stories, ideals and lessons are passed on from generation to generation. Abraham is a father who all men should strive to be like.

Abraham made many mistakes but he possessed great faith. Abraham is credited for fathering a nation through Isaac. There is actually a nation of people living today that can trace their history back to one man, Father Abraham. We can even say that Abraham fathered many more nations through his son Ishmael. Stories about Abraham were passed down to each generation making Abraham a legendary father.

- The Conclusion

I am charging you to be a Legendary Man in every aspect. You will never reach the pinnacle of manhood, so strive to keep growing as a man. Whether you are 10 years old reading this book or 90 years old, let your search for manhood be continuous.

Let the lessons I learned growing up teach you how not to fall into the same traps I fell into without a father. Ultimately, each decision you make is yours to make and you have to take full responsibility for each one. That is a mark of manhood. After reading this book you can no longer put the blame on your absentee father.

You are now held to a higher standard of manhood. Let your maturity, not your age, determine where you are in your search for manhood. You must desire to be a better man than you were the day before. You can even strive to be a better man than your father ever was. That is my hope for my sons, that they would out do me in every area of their lives.

It's a new day for whomever just read this book. If you are a young man without a father, grow and become the man that you are supposed to be. If you are a single mother reading this book, encourage your son to build relationships with strong, secure men who will help him grow as a man.

Moms, with discretion, please seek to mend the relationship between your child and their biological father. If you know that the child's father is a bad influence and will be unsafe to the child, then keep the child safe and encourage the father to improve his state. And mom, please remember that you have to come to a point where you consider your sons to be "men" instead of still being "your child." When they become adults, treat them with respect and not as if they are still children. He will always be your son, but he cannot be your child forever.

Now, I leave one last charge to the fathers who have not been present in their children's lives. It is not too late to make an impact. I met my biological father when I was 30 years old – a year before I started writing this book. I have forgiven him for not being there. Today, we have a blossoming relationship.

If this is your story, give your child time to heal and get used to the idea of you being around. However, it is important that you make sure you remain consistent. Your role is to be a support and not an authority, unless you have won the child's trust. Nevertheless, the lessons you have learned, you can teach your child even if you are reunited late in life.

Lastly, to my sons, I want you to know that I love you with everything in me. All three of you have been a joy and encouragement in my life. My hope is for you to outgrow me, to become better than me in every way.

Isaiah, Nathaniel and Gabriel, keep striving to be great men and you will grow to be legendary. Love God, treat everyone, especially women, with respect. Respect yourself and your body. Remember that you are a gift to one special woman, so keep your purity until you are married to her. Never let discouragement dictate the pace of your life and, when opposition comes, make sure to charge through it with an iron fist.

You are all special young men and I am looking forward to seeing you grow up, attend and finish college, get married, find a job and make me a grandfather. I love you all. May this book guide you, my sons. May it guide all who read it.

A message from my father to young fathers,

Second chances may apply to many things in life, but I assure you missing your children grow up is not one of them. I am one of those parents who regrets not being around while mine were growing to be the beautiful adults that they are today.

The feeling is a kind of guilty regret that will eat at your morality forever. You never can get over it. I advise all young fathers and fathers to not abandon your children because they will need you in their lives.

Don't put yourself in a position to wish for a second chance that will never ever happen.

I thank God that my children do not show absolute hatred toward me.

Irving Rivera

Andre D. Harrison

ABOUT THE AUTHOR

Andre D. Harrison is an advocate for youth and families with over 12 years of experience working with children, youth and families in religious, educational and social service settings. Andre has dedicated his life to helping others, even at his own expense. Andre desires to see broken relationships between father and child restored. His ultimate goal: to eradicate fatherlessness.

Andre has also served as a pastor to youth and family in Staten Island, NY. He desires to see youth find God at a young age and cultivate a genuine understanding about Jesus and His gift of salvation. Andre is also founder and director of The ROLE Call, and organization focused on increasing Fatherhood Engagement.

He is the father of three sons. He is very passionate about his children and has proven that he will not allow anything to come before his kids.

For more information on Andre D. Harrison, visit his website at www.therolecall.org. Connect with Andre D. Harrison through www.facebook.com/therolecall and www.twitter.com/iplaymyrole.

Made in the USA
Middletown, DE
19 November 2014